The Chartered Engineering Manager

Copyright © 2020 Zulk Shamsuddin, PhD

GAFM ACADEMY

All rights reserved.

ISBN: 9798301218392

INTRODUCTION

The **Chartered Engineering Manager ™ (Ch.EM)** is a world-class certification accredited by The American Academy of Project Management ®. This credential is for individuals with skills and experience in project management, overseeing engineering operations, management of engineering facilities, managing team of engineers, managing departmental budget, managing project risks, safety compliance, business communication, and leadership management skills.

It forms the basis of the assessment that applicants must pass to gain the Chartered Engineering Manager status and inclusion in the Directory of Certified Professionals of The Global Academy of Finance and Management ®.

Stand out from the crowd with the GAFM® Chartered Engineering Manager certification and apply the designation "Ch.EM" after your name.

Who must read this book?

Engineering Manager, Engineering Consultant, Strategy Consultant, Head of Engineering Department, Civil Engineer, Electrical Engineer, Mechanical Engineer, Quantity Surveyor, or anyone who wants to get certified as the Chartered Engineering Manager.

- Golden opportunity for Graduates and Professionals.
- Getting shortlist for a job opportunity.
- Applicants with a certified credential are usually the preferred choice among top recruiters and employers.
- Candidate with certification earn attractive compensation package comparatively with others with similar job.
- Recognized credibility.
- Greater employment prospects across the globe.
- Leveraging international quality accreditation (ISO Standards) to your name, and CV.
- Get recognition of your skills and competencies as specified on the accredited endorsement training certificate.
- Leveraging the certification card to establish professional relationship during social networking, corporate events, seminars, conferences, trainings, et cetera.
- Get listed in the GAFM® Directory of Certified/Chartered Professionals.

Certification will differentiate you from the crowd, from thousands of applications eyeing on that single job opening, your profile stands tall above the rest! You will be asking yourself – what makes you so special? How could a single piece of paper make a difference? What about the bachelor's degree certificate? Some of the candidates are better than you but why aren't they shortlisted?

You may think that since you have secured a job, getting certified is optional. Think again!! When you are out of job for whatever reasons, retrenchment, corporate downsizing, economic downturn, office politics, et cetera then you start to feel the pressure to secure another job. Competition is intense out there, connections come handy but not everyone has strong cable these days. When you look at job adverts, although they did not explicitly mention that you must be certified to apply for the job opening, they do filter candidates based on these criteria when it comes to shortlist thousands of candidates.

So, you are left out of the opportunity to compete in the job marketplace! Then you start rushing to get certified. It's a little too late. By that time, the certification fee has gone up.

If you do not have working experience then it is highly unlikely you will be offered to sit for any certification courses. This put fresh graduates in a highly difficult position. If you have the ambition to work abroad, you need to have at least one accredited and globally recognized certification to apply for jobs abroad being in the US, Europe, Middle East or elsewhere. If you don't have this, it is highly unlikely that you will get your application shortlisted.

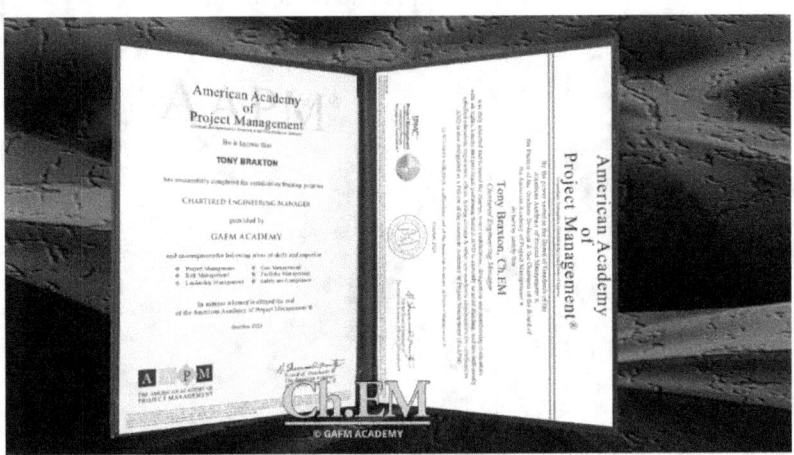

(actual certificates in your name with certified seal emblem)

THE VALUE OF CERTIFICATION

- Certification helps in learning new technologies, skills, and abilities for a specific promotion. Earning a new certification or an advanced certification in a particular area of expertise can help in advancing your career.

- Professional certification shows consumers and potential employers that you are committed to your profession and are well-trained. It gives them confidence in your abilities and knowledge. Certification makes you more valuable to employers, so you can expect to earn more than someone without certification.

- Certifications can give you the chance to learn needed skills, and be a quick way to show employers you have those skills. On the other hand, certifications can require studying or coursework, and cost up to several hundred dollars to take.

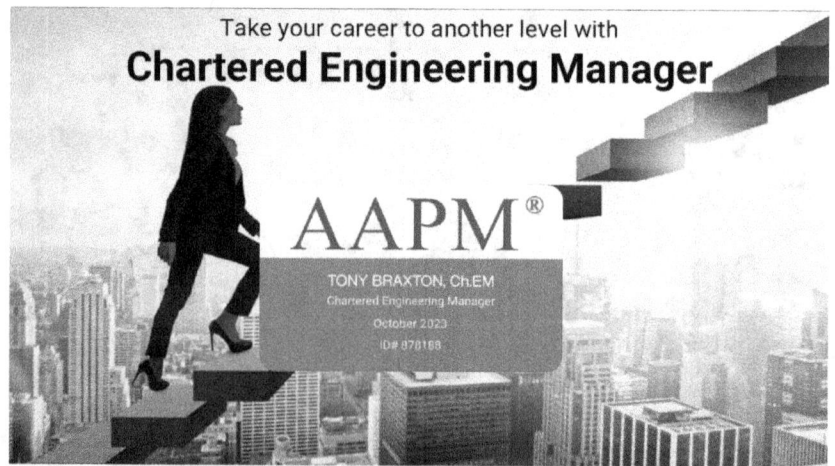

Take Your Career to Another Level

When you have the professional knowledge you need, a certification allows you to prove it. Certifications indicate mastery of skills or standards. Professional certifications are granted by industry groups or career-related organizations. These groups assess your qualifications, usually through an exam or application process. Many certifications include the privilege to use a related designation following your professional title. A professional certification differs from a license, which permits you to work in a certain profession and is usually issued by government or regulatory agencies.

Certification is about verifying your experience against a set of skills and competencies that are related to the specific job or role. Obviously you need to have the appropriate level of knowledge associated with the skills. You also need to have the minimum qualification (bachelor degree) and higher as a prerequisite for any certification.

KNOWLEDGE + QUALIFICATION + EXPERIENCE

are the cornerstones of GAFM® Certifications

Examination is not only based upon your knowledge, skills and competencies but also the methodologies, processes, and the industry standards that you need to know and practice in your past experience. At GAFM Academy, we provide an eBook to facilitate the examination process so that the assessments are aligned with the skills and competencies pertaining to the specific certification.

Engineering Manager Skills

The skills you look for in an engineering manager depend on their expertise. If you're searching for an entry-level engineering manager, they will be less skilled than experts.

Here are some skills to consider when you hire engineering managers.

Analytical Skills

Engineering managers have to deal with complex problems. They may have to find new ways to solve problems or improve processes. Thus, they need strong analytical skills to understand these issues and develop solutions. For example, in IT, an engineering manager might have to solve a problem with a new software application. If they take too long, the company risks losing money. Likewise, if they fail to solve the problem, it can result in production delays.

Detail-Oriented

In engineering, even minor errors can cause huge problems. That's why engineering managers must be detail-oriented. They have to check the work of their subordinates to ensure that it meets all the requirements. If they miss something, it can result in costly mistakes.

Leadership Skills

An engineering manager must be able to lead a team of engineers. The manager has to motivate them and ensure that they work together efficiently. Otherwise, the team will be unable to meet deadlines or produce high-quality work.

Communication Skills

Engineering managers need strong communication skills to explain technical problems to non-engineers. They must also communicate the company's goals to their team and get them on board. For example, many engineering managers have to work with sales teams. Since the sales team is not engineering-savvy, the manager must be able to explain the features of a new product in layman's terms.

Math Skills

Calculus and other math skills are a must for engineering managers. These skills help them understand complex problems and develop solutions. Engineering managers also have to create budgets for projects. So, they need to be good with numbers and understand financial reports.

Organizational Skills

An engineering manager must be well-organized to juggle multiple projects simultaneously. They have to create schedules, assign tasks, and track the progress of each project. All of this can be pretty overwhelming. However, engineering managers must be able to keep everything under control.

Technical Skills

The technical skills of an engineering manager depend on their area of expertise. For example, managers of electrical engineers need to know about circuit design principles. Likewise, managers of software engineers need to be familiar with coding languages. Some engineering managers are experts in their field. Others have a general understanding of engineering concepts.

Interpersonal Skills

Since engineering managers have to deal with people, they need strong interpersonal skills. They must be able to build relationships and resolve conflicts. Moreover, they should be able to give constructive feedback.

Click the link below

https://shorturl.at/cES36

FREQUENTLY ASKED QUESTIONS

Why do I need to submit a CV?

We only accept candidates who meet the minimum qualification requirements and credible work experience.

When will GAFM process my application?

Application will only be processed after payment is received.

How do I pay?

We accept payments via Credit / Debit card. Payment link will be shared once your application has been accepted.

Can I pay via bank wire transfer?

Yes, we will share the invoice with banking details.

How do I prepare myself for the exam?

This is a self-study model. An eBook will be provided, examination will be based on the information in the eBook. The eBook will be provided FREE to successful candidates after payment has been made.

How long is the duration of self-study period?

You must complete this study period inclusive of the exam within ten days from the date of payment.

How do I write the exam?

When you're ready to write the exam, kindly email us to book your schedule for the exam.

How do I apply for exemption from the exam?

This is at the discretion of the Board. You may be requested to submit additional information in addition to the CV submitted earlier. In any case, if your experience is good, we will apply for an exemption only after payment has been received.

How is the exam structured?

The examination comprised of 40 multiple choice questions.
Difficulty: Moderate   Duration: 60 minutes

What is the passing grade?

70%

When will I know the result of the exam?

Within 48 hours

What if I failed in the first attempt?

You are allowed to rewrite the exam without any additional charge.

When will I receive the certification documents?

Shipping is within 10 business days after you complete the course.

What courier services do we use?

We ship via United Parcel Service / FedEx

What are the certification documents?

i) professional accredited certificate   ii) endorsement training certificate   iii) certification card

Can I get a digital copy of the certificates?

We do not issue digital copy.

What is the endorsement training certificate?

This is the certificate that indicate the skills and competencies associated with the professional accredited certificate where you have accomplished via the online training program.

Can I apply the designation after my name while waiting for the certification documents?

Yes

Chapter 1 : REQUIREMENTS ENGINEERING

WHAT IS REQUIREMENTS ENGINEERING?

A requirement is a necessary attribute in a system, a statement that identifies a capability, characteristic, or quality factor of a system in order for it to have value and utility to a customer or user. Requirements are important because they provide the basis for all of the development work that follows. Once the requirements are set, developers initiate the other technical work: system design, development, testing, implementation, and operation. Too often, there is a tendency to want to start what is often referred to as "the real work" (developing, or programming, the software) too quickly. Many customers and project managers (PMs) seem to believe that actual programming work ("coding") indicates that progress is being made. According to industry experience, insufficient time and effort are spent on the requirements-related activities associated with system development. Industry experience confirms that a better approach is to invest more time in requirements gathering, analysis, and management activities. The reason is that, typically, coding work is started much sooner than it should be because additional time is needed to identify the "real" requirements and to plan for requirements-related activities.

REQUIREMENTS ENGINEERING

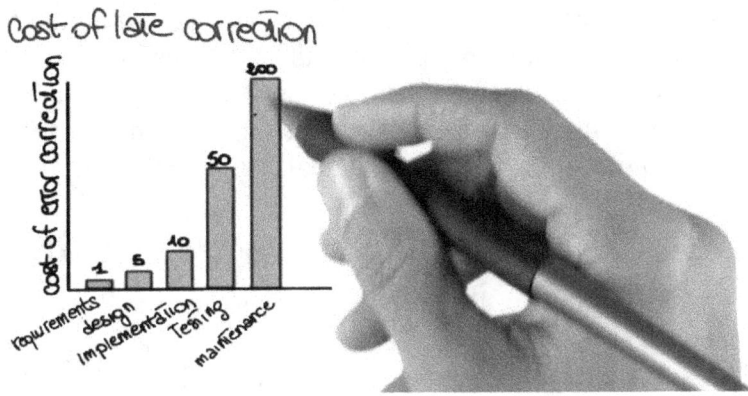

There is a significant difference between "stated" requirements and "real" requirements. Stated requirements are those provided by a customer at the beginning of a system or software development effort, for example, in a request for information, proposal, or quote or in a statement of work (SOW). Real requirements are those that reflect the verified needs of users for a particular system or capability. There is often a huge difference between the stated requirements and the real requirements. Analysis of the stated requirements is required to determine and refine real customer and user needs and expectations of the delivered system. The requirements need to be filtered by a process of clarification of their meaning and identification of other aspects that need to be considered. To cite a simple example, requirements analysts (RAs) are more familiar with the need to state requirements clearly. There are many ways in which the capability, understanding, and communication of the meaning of each and every requirement may be different to a user than to a developer. Therefore, it is vital (and time saving) that all requirements be clarified through the mechanism of a joint customer/user and RA effort. Customers and users need the support of technically trained and experienced professionals, and vice versa, to ensure effective communication. Developers need to have that same understanding so that the solution they define addresses the needs in the way everyone expects. Misunderstandings of requirements result in wasted effort and rework. Another important insight is that sometimes the requirements are unknowable at the outset of a development effort because they are affected by the new capabilities to be provided in the new system. This suggests the need to plan for new and changed requirements to provide a degree of flexibility.

ENGINEERING REQUIREMENTS DOCUMENT (ERD)

An Engineering Requirements Document (ERD) is a statement describing the goal and purpose of a new component. Unlike a Product Requirements Document (PRD), which tells engineers what they need to build, an Engineering Requirements Document specifies why a part is being built and how its design fuels its purpose. By following the engineering requirements outlined in an Engineering Requirements Document, engineers can ensure that the part they build will satisfy customer needs. Using an Engineering Requirements Document also helps streamline production in various ways:

- Engineering Requirements Document use defined and consistent communication to promote collaboration, reduce miscommunication, and keep everyone on the same page.
- Engineering Requirements Document help break down large projects into smaller tasks, making them easier to delegate or outsource.
- Engineering Requirements Document can be checked against PRDs to ensure all design intentions are correctly implemented and all product goals are achieved.

A well-written Engineering Requirements Document allows engineers and manufacturers to answer critical questions about part design and purpose without going back and forth. This results in a faster, more efficient building process that saves you time and money. Here's everything you need to know to write a clear and effective engineering requirements document. Standard criteria for an engineering requirements document. To start, all effective engineering requirements documents have the following six elements in common:

Clarity

All engineering requirements should be clear, short, and unambiguous in order to avoid confusion. Less is more often, a one-sentence description will suffice.

Necessity

To avoid confusion or contradictions, only put the absolutely essential requirements in your Engineering Requirements Document. Determine the worst-case scenario for each requirement and if there aren't any consequences, there's no need for it to be in your Engineering Requirements Document.

Coordination

Engineering requirements should be correct throughout product design. An Engineering Requirements Document should describe all product requirements, goals, conditions, and capabilities. Whenever possible, explain what the product does in a numerical manner for the most precision.

Testability

Whenever you write a new engineering requirement, you must be able to verify a successful implementation. There are many different kinds of testing methods to ensure verifiability, including inspection, user testing, software testing, and system integration testing. Choose the testing method that makes the most sense for your project.

Feasibility

Stay within the limits of what can be achieved technically, as well as what is legally, organizationally, and financially possible. Be reasonable and honest, since creating non-feasible requirements will cause complications down the line. If feasibility can't be reached, you can state a design detail as a goal rather than a requirement.

Traceability

Any engineer looking at your Engineering Requirements Document should be able to trace each requirement back to the original product's purpose. Linking implementations back to product goals helps explain why an element is important, where it's coming from, and how it makes sense with the overall part design.

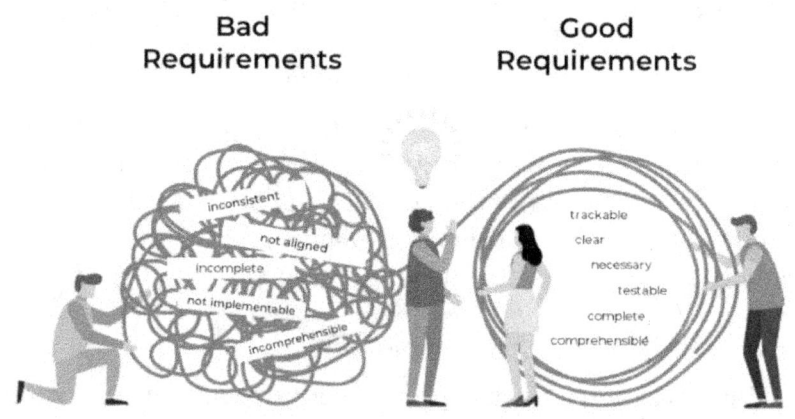

TIPS FOR WRITING A GOOD ENGINEERING REQUIREMENTS DOCUMENT

Once you've made sure that the standard criteria have been accounted for, you can implement best practices that will take your engineering requirements document to the next level. Here are five tips for writing a top-notch engineering requirements document.

USE AN ENGINEERING REQUIREMENTS TEMPLATE

You can save time and energy at the beginning of a new project by using an engineering requirements document template. An Engineering Requirements Document template ensures your Engineering Requirements Document is always properly structured. At a minimum, an engineering requirements document template should have a cover page, section headings, and other standardized sections known as "boilerplates." Use boilerplates to cover Engineering Requirements Document topics like verb use, abbreviations, keywords, formatting standards, and other guidelines necessary for understanding your Engineering Requirements Document.

AVOID WRITING OPERATIONS AND IMPLEMENTATIONS

Your engineering requirements should state a goal, not how the goal will be achieved. If you explain the steps towards completing a purpose instead of the purpose itself, you're not really writing an Engineering Requirements Document you're writing an operations and implementation guide. If you write an operations and implementations guide by mistake, a manufacturer might misunderstand your intentions and your project goals might not be met.

To ensure your requirements are indeed requirements, ask yourself why this requirement is a necessary part of your engineering requirements document. Trust that the system designers and manufacturers will determine how the goal will be achieved and that they'll do so in the most efficient way possible.

EVALUATE YOUR ENGINEERING REQUIREMENTS DOCUMENT

This will help verify that all engineering requirements meet your stated goals and company aspirations. For a well-rounded evaluation, it's best to put together a diverse team. This includes bringing people of all races, ethnicities, and genders together to evaluate your engineering requirements document, but also includes bringing a diversity of roles to the evaluation. Include as many roles as you can designers, developers, testers, end-user representatives, those in charge of maintenance and management, and of course the client team to bring plenty of valuable insights to your Engineering Requirements Document evaluation.

DON'T BE OVERLY SPECIFIC

Although there are a lot of language rules to follow when writing your engineering requirements document, keep it simple. Clarity is key for Engineering Requirements Document, so only focus on the necessary goals, objectives, and constraints of your requirement. Always have a reason for putting in a requirement too many requirements will muddle your Engineering Requirements Document and confuse readers. If you feel your requirements becoming too long and complicated, use bullet points to split up its elements. Having a well-written Engineering Requirements Document will help engineers, product teams, and other collaborators better understand your design intentions. By clearly connecting a component's design to its specific goals and overall part purpose, an Engineering Requirements Document ensures a product is built in a way to satisfy customer needs.

Most importantly, a great Engineering Requirements Document promotes collaboration, communication, and clarity throughout the design and manufacturing process. This will ensure each and every part is fully functional and will complete its desired objectives. Along with ensuring part-to-part consistency, an Engineering Requirements Document also promotes faster production runs and lower costs.

Managers often think of requirements-related activities as consisting primarily of gathering requirements and managing changes to those requirements. In reality, there are several other requirements-related activities that need to be addressed in the system life cycle:

IDENTIFYING THE STAKEHOLDERS

This includes anyone who has an interest in the system or in its possessing qualities that meet particular needs. Gaining an understanding of the customers' and users' needs for the planned system and their expectations of it: This is often referred to as requirements elicitation. Note that the requirements can include several types.

REQUIREMENTS GATHERING TECHNIQUES

- **Identifying requirements:** This involves stating requirements in simple sentences and providing them as a set. Business needs or requirements are the essential activities of an enterprise. They are derived from business goals (the objectives of the enterprise). Business scenarios may be used as a technique for understanding business requirements. A key factor in the success of a system is the extent to which it supports the business requirements and facilitates an organization in achieving them.

- **Clarifying and restating the requirements:** This is done to ensure that they describe the customer's real needs and are in a form that can be understood and used by developers of the system.

- **Analyzing the requirements:** This is done to ensure that they are well defined and that they conform to the criteria of a good requirement.

- **Defining the requirements** in a way that means the same thing to all of the stakeholders. Note that each stakeholder group may have a significantly different perspective of the system and the system's requirements. Sometimes this requires investing significant time learning a special vocabulary or project lexicon. Often it requires spending considerable time and effort to achieve a common understanding.

- **Specifying the requirements**: This requires including all of the precise detail of each requirement so that it can be included in a specification document or other documentation, depending on the size of the project.

- **Prioritizing the requirements**: All requirements are not of equal importance to the customers and users of the planned system. Some are critical, some of relatively high priority, some of normal or average priority, and some even of lower priority. It is important to prioritize all of the requirements because there is never enough time or money to do everything we'd like to do in our developed systems. Prioritizing the requirements provides the opportunity to address the highest priority first and possibly release a version of a product that addresses lower-priority needs. Prioritizing helps ensure that an appropriate amount of investment is made in meeting various customer needs.

- **Deriving requirements**: There are some requirements that come about because of the design of a system, but do not provide a direct benefit to the end user. A requirement for disc storage might result from the need to store a lot of data, for example.

- **Partitioning requirements**: We categorize requirements as those that can be met by hardware, software, training, and documentation, for example. Often this process turns out to be more complex than we anticipate when some requirements are satisfied by more than one category.

- **Allocating requirements**: We allocate requirements to different subsystems and components of the system. The allocations may not always be satisfied by just one subsystem or component.

- **Tracking requirements**: We need the capability to trace or track where in the system each requirement is satisfied, so that we can verify that each requirement is being addressed. This is most often accomplished through use of an automated requirements tool.
- **Managing requirements**: We need to be able to add, delete, and modify requirements during all of the phases of system design, development, integration, testing, deployment, and operation. The requirements repository consists of a set of artifacts and databases.
- **Testing and Verifying requirements**: This are the process of checking requirements, designs, code, test plans, and system products to ensure that the requirements are met.
- **Validating requirements**: This is the process for confirming that the real requirements are implemented in the delivered system. The order of validation of requirements should be prioritized since there is a limited amount of funding available.

TYPES OF REQUIREMENTS

It's important for the RA or requirements engineer to settle on definitions of the types of requirements that he will use consistently. He should advocate consistent meanings for these types on his project and in his organization. Much confusion can be avoided by agreeing on a set of definitions and by not using certain terms. In this chapter, we'll review several types of requirements and suggest definitions for them. We'll suggest why some terms shouldn't be used and provide other guidelines. One important reason for agreeing on the definitions of the types of requirements is to avoid lengthy and heated debates about terminology while we are working together. Establish a project glossary that everyone can live with (even if some definitions are not everyone's favorites) and utilize it in your work.

A requirement is a statement that identifies a capability, characteristic, or quality factor of a system in order for it to have value and utility for a user. A requirement is well-defined and more specific than a need, which is a capability desired by a user or customer to solve a problem or achieve an objective.

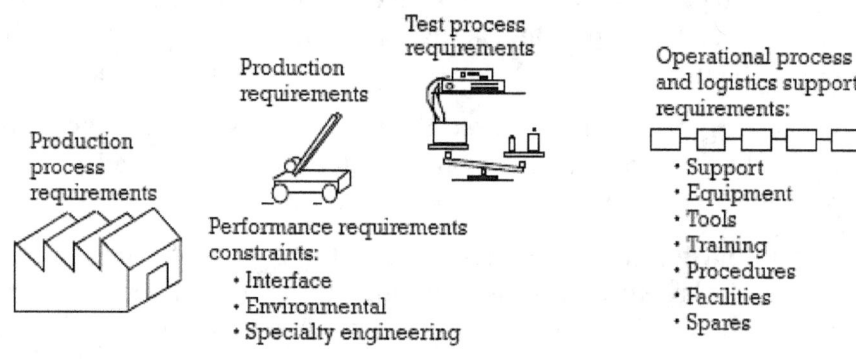

The requirements types that are noted are production process requirements (e.g., the physical facilities needed), requirements of the products to be provided by the system or software, the requirements of the processes utilized to produce the products (e.g., the testing process), and operational and logistics support requirements (e.g., equipment, training, and procedures). All of these requirements must be identified before work on the detailed system design is started. While the product engineers are developing specifications for the product elements, the manufacturing engineers must define the manufacturing requirements, the logistics engineers the logistics requirements, and the verification engineers the qualification requirements. While doing so, these engineers must communicate among themselves and jointly resolve the best aggregate expression of the requirements from the product and process perspective.

Business Requirements

Business requirements are the reason for developing systems and software in the first place. Business requirements are the essential activities of an enterprise. Business requirements are derived from business goals (the objectives of the enterprise or organization). Business scenarios may be used as a technique for understanding business requirements. A key factor in the success of a system is the extent to which the system supports the business requirements and facilitates an organization in achieving them. If our systems and software do not support the business requirements effectively and efficiently, they have no reason for being.

High-Level or System-Level Requirements

To enable comprehending a needed system, we refer to the high-level or system-level requirements. This term relates to those requirements that are foremost in importance, capture the vision of the customer, enable defining the scope of the system, and allow estimating the cost and schedule required to build the system. (Some system architects believe that the requirements specification should contain every performance requirement.) It's recommended that a workable number of requirements (on the order of 50 to 200) system-level requirements be identified for a large system.

Functional Requirements

Functional requirements are an important category of the real requirements. Functional requirements describe what the system or software must do. A function is a useful capability provided by one or more components of a system. Functional requirements are sometimes called behavioral or operational requirements because they specify the inputs to the system, the outputs (responses) from the system, and behavioral relationships between them. The document used to communicate the requirements to customers, system, and software engineers is referred to as a functional document (FD) or specification. This refers to a comprehensive collection of the characteristics of a system and the capabilities it will make available to the users. It provides a detailed analysis of the data the system will be expected to manipulate. It may include a detailed definition of the user interfaces of the system.

DERIVED REQUIREMENTS

A derived requirement is one that is further refined from a higher-level requirement or a requirement that results from choosing a specific implementation or system element. In a sense, all requirements are derived from the system need; thus, the derived distinction tends to have little significance. However, many systems engineers distinguish between externally identified requirements and requirements that are derived under the control of the engineer.

DESIGN REQUIREMENTS AND DESIGN CONSTRAINTS

For most system development efforts, design requirements/constraints appear right at the beginning of the system formulation. Here are examples of why it's difficult to separate requirements engineering from design activities:

- New systems are often installed in environments that already have other systems. The other systems usually constrain the design of the new system. For example, a requirement (design constraint) may be that the system to be developed must obtain its information from an existing database. The database has already been designed and parts of its specification will usually be included in the requirements document.

- For large systems, some architectural design is often necessary to identify subsystems and relationships. Identifying subsystems means that the requirements engineering process for each subsystem can go on in parallel.

- For reasons of budget, schedule, or quality, an organization may wish to reuse some or all existing software systems in the implementation of a new system. This constrains both the system requirements and the design.
- If a system has to be approved by an external regulator (e.g., systems in civil aircraft), it may be necessary to use standard certified design that has been tested in other systems.

ENVIRONMENTAL REQUIREMENTS

These are requirements that result from the physical setting and social and cultural conditions of the system development effort and the setting in which the system or software will be used.

SYSTEM, SUBSYSTEM, AND COMPONENT REQUIREMENTS

This refers to requirements associated with different levels of the system. The system is the highest level and is divided into subsystems; the subsystems are made up of components, such as hardware, software, training, and documentation.

KEY REQUIREMENTS

The term key requirements are sometimes used to refer to requirements that are important in order to understand a system's essential capabilities or functions. 4 It is appropriate to analyze requirements in terms of their benefit-to-cost ratio, risk, or the estimated time and effort needed to address them, so that we can have informal discussions within the joint team to negotiate the requirements to be included. However, I suggest avoiding use of this term, because it's unclear.

GATHERING REQUIREMENTS

The need to gather requirements is initiated by a request from an internal or external customer. Requests can come in many forms, including a request for proposals, an SOW, or an informal or formal inquiry describing a capability that is needed. The request initiates a set of requirements-gathering activities. It's vital for the RA to have a thorough understanding of these activities and to gain experience in performing related tasks.

A lot of time and effort is wasted in the project startup phase and in performing requirements gathering activities. There are a number of reasons for this:

- The project is just getting organized and things are confused.
- There is no road map or checklist of startup activities.
- Not all staff are present; some are still being recruited.
- There isn't much pressure to meet the schedule yet.
- The customer and users are also trying to get organized and get started.
- The staff who will be working on end-product development may not fully understand the customer's objectives and, consequently, may not be able to appreciate the customer's expectations.
- An effective proven procedure for the requirements gathering steps is not available or used.

Chapter 2 : FACILITIES MANAGEMENT

Facilities management strategy is a tool for facility management that focuses on improving the workplace to boost productivity, performance and well-being of workers in a company. For efficient and effective services, facilities management strategy allows the deeper understanding of the needs of an organization or business and places procedures and processes to meet these needs.

The right strategy goes beyond providing day to day support and service and starts creating long term initiatives that can sustain the life of assets and improve productivity. The driving force behind a facilities management strategy is the safety and happiness of the people in the facility.

WHAT IS FACILITY MANAGEMENT?

Facility management refers to how facilities at an organization are managed and maintained. These facilities are not limited to offices but can also include mechanical and electrical utilities or the company's physical resources with the potential to cause the employees a safety or health hazard. Facility management is affected by technology changes and advancements imploring facility managers to identify technology investments that can positively influence facilities management.

WHAT IS A FACILITIES MANAGEMENT STRATEGY?

Facilities management strategy is a collaboration between facility management and facility planning focusing on long term outcomes and involves incorporating facility management into company initiatives. Facilities management strategy calls for an understanding of business goals and linking them to facility management to improve the workplace and organization. It's driven by goals.

Why Is Facility Management More Relevant Than Ever?

Facility management can ensure that companies are running efficiently and effectively. Buildings with a facility management team run properly as they are responsible for the day-to-day analysis of utilities at the company as well as maintenance and repairs. They also take part in strategic planning activities of the company to aid the growth of employee productivity and cut down costs.

Studies have shown that the best workplace environment can affect productivity and improve the well-being of workers which can affect business output and the success of organizations as a whole. For example, clean working space and bathrooms can make workers feel comfortable and secure. Facilities management takes care of such services. With skilled management experts and your own facilities manager, we can offer you tailor-made management services both on a short or long-term basis so you can focus on other aspects of your business without worry.

What are Facility Management's objectives?

Facility management involves so many responsibilities that include ensuring comfort, functionality, safety and happiness of occupants in a building that is being managed. To successfully accomplish all these, there are facility management objectives that should be met and these objectives can fit all types of facilities.

Communication with Stakeholders and Occupants

For everything to run smoothly as you manage a building, establish and maintain communication with occupants and stakeholders of the building. Such dialogue can help you learn how they view the facility and they can also offer invaluable suggestions to make the environment more comfortable and safer.

For every facility that Busters Group is offering facility management to, our team invents an easy but vital system for communication for occupants to tell us their recommendations and opinions on how the job should be done better so every occupant is happy and feels secure.

Provide a Safe and Healthy Environment

Safety is always our main concern here at Busters Group. By being aware of potential health risks and creating strategies to correct and avoid some of these risks we can keep a lot of people safe. In buildings that we are managing, we focus on bathrooms because they are an essential part of any building. By maintaining cleanliness, freshness and stocking them with adequate toiletries we make them as pleasant as possible for every visit made. Our team also focuses on reducing the level of moisture and mold growth in bathrooms by doing regular inspections on stalls and investing in high-density polyethene that not only improves the quality of air but also prevents mold growth.

Be Mindful of Deficiencies

Some things if left unchecked for a long time can ultimately affect the functionality of utilities in a building. Routine checks can help identify any building deficiencies and avoid bigger problems in future. A facility manager is responsible to make these routine checks every three to 6 months.

Improve and Endorse Energy Efficiency

Making the facility more energy-efficient can save money. By going over the expenses of the building on water, gas and electricity a manager can identify how much is being spent and ways of reducing energy wastage. Investing in equipment that can save energy such as energy-efficient light bulbs, boosting existing equipment and sealing off leaks on pipes can reduce and prevent more wastage of energy.

What Are The 5 Steps in Strategic Facility Planning?

Strategic facility planning (SFP) is a key process that can enhance the delivery of services from a facility management team to its stakeholders. An SFP can reduce delays and customer dissatisfaction with services being offered and ensures that all facility management activities are in line with the corporate direction of the business. With SFP a facility manager can help organizations become effective and conducive space for workers. The process follows these steps:

1) Clarify Your Strategic Position

To know the right needs of a facility, an analysis of the current position or conditions of the building must be done. The team must study the values, culture, vision and goals of the organization they want to work with and develop strategies that will be in line with these core values. The facility manager must understand where the organization is heading, what changes might occur and how they will affect the real estate needs of the organization. This can help predict future needs, requirements and costs for operations, maintenance and space.

2) Prioritize Your Objectives

After identifying the needs, a facility manager must evaluate the objectives that collaborate with the core values and vision of the organization and how each chosen objective can help reach set goals. Priority should be given to objectives that are more urgent, relate more to the needs of stakeholders and can support the performance of everyone at the workplace.

3) Formulate A Strategy

Formulating a strategy involves identifying the right initiatives to reach set objectives and creating a time frame to reach them.

4) Implement and Manage the Strategy

With the plan on paper, it can be implemented, but for its success, everyone in the organization must be aware of what sort of strategies you have put in place. Team members should know what their roles will be throughout the facility management plan.

5) Monitor and Evaluate Strategy

To determine if the strategy is successful, continue to monitor the work being done and check if progress matches up with set priorities. Managers can also take opinions from members of the organization to see if the work they are providing is up to their standards. Where priorities or changes must be made in approach, the manager is also responsible for these.

IMPLEMENTING STRATEGIC FACILITY MANAGEMENT

It takes control to perfectly carry out strategic facility management. The International Facility Management Association list's four steps to successfully implement a strategic facility plan:

Understand

Strategic facility management is guided by goals and the capacity of facilities to support such goals. The strategy must be well understood before it is executed and this goes beyond knowing the time frame to identifying if the strategy has enough resources to run.

Analyze

The second step in facilities management calls for a deeper understanding and experimentation on how the plan can be put into action. Use experimental and analytic tools to help fully build the strategy. By using scenario planning you can have a systematic layout of the plan and to analyze focus areas we use SWOT (Strengths, Weaknesses, opportunities and Threats) analysis. Brainstorming and Strategic Creative Analysis (SCAN) can help the whole team come up with facility improvement ideas.

Plan

Developing a strategic facility plan is easy after outlining what you want to do and how to do it. A facility manager is usually the one who hands in this physical plan to executive managers for approval. The plan details what changes should be made to the facility, why they should happen and what will be done for such changes to occur. Like a business plan, the facility plan shows the time frame for actions, responsibilities of team members and shows how success will be measured.

Act

After the plan is approved, it's time for action. Strategic facility management requires leaders that can execute the changes in line with the strategic management facilities plan and who are able to track and report changes and improvements to the overall plan. These leaders should value the vision at the facilities level and know how it affects the goals of the business. After implementation, continue to measure the success of the strategy on different aspects of the business.

BUSINESS CONTINUITY PLANNING

Some facilities depend on fully functioning equipment to run. A business continuity plan is like a contingency plan that identifies the key assets of a facility and the potential risks that the asset has. The plan also shows how business operations could be affected if the asset stopped functioning. With evaluation and the right plan, you can ensure that a business or facility does not stop its operations if the inevitable should occur.

Facilities management is the process by which an organization ensures that its buildings, systems, and services support the organization's core operations and processes as well as contribute to achieving its strategic objectives in changing conditions. It focuses resources on meeting user needs to support the key role of people in organizations and strives to continuously improve quality, reduce risks and ensure value for money. It is an important management function and business service. Major organizations worldwide are using it as part of their strategy for restructuring to provide a competitive edge. It can also ensure that buildings and support services improve customer responsiveness and contribute to business objectives.

The scope of the discipline covers all aspects of property, space, environmental control, health and safety, and support services, and requires that appropriate control points are established in the organization. The facilities management plan will set out these policies and identify corporate guidelines and standards. It will describe the organization, its structure, procedures and responsibilities. Facilities management policies lay out an organization's response to vital issues such as space allocation and charging, environmental control and protection, and direct and contract employment. The policies will set a direction for the organization and establish the values of and attitudes toward the facilities users including the corporation, its operating units and customers, individual employees and the public.

Facilities management entails the integration of people, technology and support services to achieve an organization's mission. It is concerned primarily with the quality of service to all stakeholders in the organization. In a service level model, the informed buyer assesses needs, agrees on the desired service levels and purchases services to meet them. The facilities organization must enable managers to focus on buying the best standard of service achievable within an agreed budget.

The primary objective of facility management is to deliver the optimum facility management services stipulated in the contractual agreement within the scope, budget, and quality requirements. The emphasis here is on management and business rather than the technical aspects of the facility management mission.

Both the organization and the facility manager should have a specific philosophy about facilities.

- Facility management is an essential business function; the facility manager is a business manager and should be placed at the same level as the managers of human relations and/or information technology.

- Different types of organizations require different approaches to facility management (and services may be provided in-house or contracted out), but there are a limited number of ways to organize depending upon the mission.

- Every FM organization will have some element contracted out so contract negotiation and administration skills are essential for every facility manager.

- Facility managers need to be innovative in their contracting. Low-bid contracts are seldom appropriate, and we must partner with our contractors and consultants while insisting that they perform if they are to continue working for us.

- Good facility management is based on the good leadership of a proper organization.
- Facility managers need to have the same level of business skills as their management colleagues.
- Facility managers must know their business both the FM business and the business they support.
- While it is improving, facility management needs better basic research and better application of both existing research and best practices.
- Facility managers are in a position where they can influence how substantial organizational resources are spent. Conduct your business with the highest degree of ethics and a sense of stewardship.
- Sustainability, security, and emergency management are functions with great management and customer interest, which every FM must accommodate.

THE FACILITY MANAGEMENT TEAM

A major challenge for the engineering manager is forming a facility management team and getting it to function as a team. Unfortunately, many factors in a company work counter to a team approach, which is why a facility manager must be a leader, not simply a manager. We have mentioned repeatedly the diverse nature of staffing in most facility departments; staff, contractors, and consultants. This allows for both maximizations of skills and flexibility to meet peak workloads. Yet all members of the team, regardless of employment status, must feel that they are important members of one team. This is true even for one-time contractors. In some organizations, even though it makes sense, a staff member is never to be placed in a position subordinate to a consultant. Bureaucratic personnel policies or traditions that preclude such assignments often run contrary to effective team building and require an aggressive leader to get them modified. In today's contractor and consultant-laden business world, this consultant may be the best (or only) person, to train, manage, and guide an employee, regardless of staffing status.

Unfortunately, some good management techniques often run contrary to good teamwork. Excessive dependence on quantitative measurement, particularly measuring one work unit against another, often leads to cutting corners, bickering, and even sabotage. Quantitative measurements always must be evaluated in context and used as indicators for discussion on ways to improve, not as the final word. Likewise, subordinate objectives must reinforce departmental goals. Successful teamwork and subordinates who stress an understanding and support of the entire organization must be rewarded.

FM Service Management

The main principle of FM service management is to ensure the FM project will meet or exceed stakeholders' needs and expectations. The FM project team must develop a good relationship with key stakeholders, especially the project sponsor and the key project stakeholders of the project, to understand what quality means to them. One of the causes for poor project evaluations is the project focuses only on meeting the written requirements for the main outputs and ignores other stakeholder needs and expectations for the project.

Quality must be viewed on an equal level with scope, schedule, and budget. If a project sponsor is not satisfied with the quality of how the project is delivering the outcomes, the project team will need to make adjustments to the scope, schedule, and budget to satisfy the project sponsor's needs and expectations. To deliver the project scope on time and within budget is not enough; to achieve stakeholder satisfaction the project must develop a good working relationship with all stakeholders and understand their stated or implied needs.

FM Quality Service Management consists of three main processes.

PLAN QUALITY MANAGEMENT

Plan Quality Management refers to the process of identifying quality requirements and standards for the project and its deliverables and documenting how the project will demonstrate compliance with quality requirements.

PERFORM QUALITY ASSURANCE

Perform Quality Assurance refers to the process of auditing the quality requirements and the results from quality control measurements to ensure that appropriate quality standards and operational definitions are used.

CONTROL QUALITY

Control Quality refers to the process of monitoring and recording results of executing quality activities to assess performance and recommend necessary changes.

FM QUALITY MANAGEMENT PLANNING

The first step in the FM quality management planning process is to define quality. The project manager and the team must identify what quality standards will be used in the project, it will look at the project sponsor, key project stakeholders, the organization and other key stakeholders to come up with a good definition of quality. In some instances, the organization or the area of specialization of the project (engineering, IT, FM, health, water, or education) may have some standard definitions of quality that can be used by the project.

Identifying quality standards is a key component of quality definition that will help identify the key characteristics that will govern project activities and ensure the key project stakeholders and project sponsors will accept the project outcomes.

Quality management implies the ability to anticipate situations and prepare actions that will help bring the desired outcomes. The goal is the prevention of defects through the creation of actions that will ensure that the project team understands what is defined as quality.

SOURCES OF QUALITY DEFINITION

One source for the definition of quality comes from the project sponsor. the project must establish conversations with the project sponsor to be familiar with and come to a common understanding of what the project sponsor defines as quality. The project sponsor may have certain standards of what is expected from the project, and how the project delivers the expected benefits to the key project stakeholders. This is in line with the project's ultimate objective that the project outcomes have the ability to satisfy the stated or implied needs.

Another source for quality definition comes from the key project stakeholders; the project team must be able to understand how the key project stakeholders define quality from their perspective, a perspective that is more focused on fitness for use, the project outcomes must be relevant to the current needs of the key project stakeholders and must result in improvements to their lives. The team can create, as part of the baseline data collection, questions that seek to understand how the key project stakeholders define the project will meet their needs and a question that also helps define what project success looks like from the perspective of a beneficiary.

The development organization may have its own quality standards that can reflect the technical and managerial nature of the project. The organization may require from the project timely and accurate delivery of project information needed for decision-making, or compliance to international or locally recognized quality standards that define specific technical areas of the project, this is quite often in health, water and nutrition projects.

FM QUALITY CHARACTERISTICS

All materials or services have characteristics that facilitate the identification of its quality. The characteristics are part of the conditions of how the material, equipment and services are able to meet the requirements of the project and are fit for use by the key project stakeholders. Quality characteristics relate to the attributes, measures and methods attached to that particular product or service.

- **Functionality** is the degree, by which equipment performs its intended function, this is important, especially for clinical equipment, that the operation should behave as expected.

- **Performance** is how well a product or service performs the key project stakeholders intended use. A water system should be designed to support extreme conditions and require little maintenance to reduce the cost to the community and increase its sustainability.

- **Reliability** represents the ability of the service or product to perform as intended under normal conditions without unacceptable failures. The material used for blood testing should be able to provide the information consistently and dependably that will help identify critical diseases. The trust of the key project stakeholders is dependent upon the quality of the tests.

- **Relevance** represents the characteristic of how a product or service meets the actual needs of the key project stakeholders, it should be pertinent, applicable, and appropriate to its intended use or application.

- **Timeliness** represents how the product or service is delivered in time to solve the problems when its needed and not after, this is a crucial characteristic for health and emergency relief work.

- **Suitability** defines the fitness of its use, its appropriateness and correctness, the agriculture equipment must be designed to operate on the sole condition the key project stakeholders will use it on.

- **Completeness** defines the quality that the service is to be completed and includes the entire scope of services. Training sessions should be completed and include all the material needed to build a desired skill or knowledge.

- **Consistency** ensures services are delivered in the same way for every beneficiary. For example, clinical tests need to be done using the same procedure for every patient.

Quality characteristics are not limited to the material, equipment or service delivered to the key project stakeholders, but also apply to the material, equipment, and services the project staff uses to deliver the project outputs. These include the vehicles, computers, various equipment, tools and consulting services the project purchases and uses to carry out its activities.

Quality characteristics must be included in all materials, equipment and services the project will purchase, the procurement officers must have a complete description of what is required by the project, otherwise, a procurement office may purchase the goods or services based on her or his information of the product.

What went wrong - A project requested the purchase of 1000 tents for a community displaced by floods, the purchase request had no specifications for its intended use (suitability), and resistance (performance). The procurement officer only knew that the tents were needed as soon as possible (timeliness), so he purchased, based on his knowledge of what a tent looks like, 1000 camping tents, they were delivered to the refugee camps on the requested timeframe, and the project manager was happy. But the next day all families that received the tents were complaining that they were not good for the cold nights and too small to accommodate their extended families. The project purchased the tents under budget and within the specified timeframe but the key project stakeholders rejected them because they did not meet their needs (quality services are poor).

FM QUALITY MANAGEMENT PLAN

A FM Quality Management Plan is a document, or several documents, that together specify quality standards, practices, resources, specifications, and the sequence of activities relevant to a particular product, service, project, or contract. FM Quality Management Plan should define:

- Objectives to be attained (for example, characteristics or specifications, uniformity, effectiveness, aesthetics, cycle time, cost, natural resources, utilization, yield, dependability, and so on).
- Steps in the processes that constitute the operating practice or procedures of the organization.
- Allocation of responsibilities, authority, and resources during the different phases of the process or project.
- Specific documented standards, practices, procedures, and instructions to be applied.
- Suitable testing, inspection, examination, and audit programs at appropriate stages.
- A documented procedure for changes and modifications to a quality plan as a process is improved.
- A method for measuring the achievement of quality objectives.
- Other actions necessary to meet the objectives.

At the highest level, quality goals and plans should be integrated with the overall strategic plans of the organization. As organizational objectives and plans are deployed throughout the organization, each function fashions its own best way of contributing to the top-level goals and objectives.

At lower levels, the quality plan assumes the role of an actionable plan. Such plans may take many different forms depending on the outcome they are to produce. Quality plans may also be represented by more than one type of document to produce a given outcome.

Part of defining quality involves developing a quality management plan and a quality checklist that will be used during the project implementation phase. This checklist will ensure the project team and other actors are delivering the project outputs according to the quality requirements.

Once the project has defined the quality standards and quality characteristics, it will create a project quality plan that describes all the quality definitions and standards relevant to the project, it will highlight the standards that must be followed to comply to regulatory requirements set up by the project sponsor, the organization and external agencies such as the local government and professional organizations (health, nutrition, etc.)

The quality plan also describes the conditions that the services and materials must possess in order to satisfy the needs and expectations of the project stakeholders, it describes the situations or conditions that make an output fall below quality standards, this information is used to gain a common understanding among the project team to help them identify what is above and what is below a quality standard.

The quality plan also includes the procedure to ensure that the quality standards are being followed by all project staff. The plan also includes the steps required to monitor and control quality and the approval process to make changes to the quality standards and the quality plan.

EXAMPLE OF A QUALITY MANAGEMENT PLAN

Let's take a look at a manufacturing company that machines metal parts. Its quality plan consists of applicable procedures that includes describing the production process and responsibilities, applicable workmanship standards, the measurement tolerances acceptable, the description of the material standards, and so forth. These may all be separate documents.

Deliverable	Quality Event	Quality Materials	Purpose
Preliminary Business Case	Expert Review	Template for Business Case Approved Business Case for Project ABC	Ensure the information is accurate and well constructed prior to submission to Steering Committee
Final Business Case	Formal Inspection by Sponsor	Template for Business Case	Ensure the Business Case is in a fit state to be submitted to the Finance Review Committee
Project Definition	Walk-through of early draft	Template for Project Definition	Review early draft for completeness
	Peer Review of final draft		Review final draft for completeness and construction
Database Design	Expert Review of physical model	Standard for Database Design	Compliance with standard General accuracy

More variable information that pertains to a particular customer may be spelled out on individual work orders. Work orders specify the machine setups and tolerances, operations to be performed, tests, inspections, handling, storing, packaging, and delivery steps to be followed.

An operating-level quality plan translates the customer requirements into actions required to produce the desired outcome and couples this with applicable procedures, standards, practices, and protocols to specify precisely what is needed, who will do it, and how it will be done. A quality control plan may specify product tolerances, testing parameters, and acceptance criteria. While the terminology may differ, the basic approach is similar for service and other types of organizations.

QUALITY ASSURANCE

Assurance is the activity of providing evidence to create confidence among all stakeholders that the quality-related activities are being performed effectively; and that all planned actions are being done to provide adequate confidence that a product or service will satisfy the stated requirements for quality.

Quality Assurance (QA) is a process to provide confirmation based on evidence to ensure to the project sponsor, key project stakeholders, organization management and other stakeholders that product meet needs, expectations, and other requirements. It assures the existence and effectiveness of process and procedures tools, and safeguards are in place to make sure that the expected levels of quality will be reached to produce quality outputs.

Quality Assurance occurs during the implementation phase of the project and includes the evaluation of the overall performance of the project on a regular basis to provide confidence that the project will satisfy the quality standards defined by the project.

Does the product or service conform to the requirements?

One of the purposes of quality management is to find errors and defects as early in the project as possible. Therefore, a good quality management process will end up taking more effort hours and cost upfront. The goal is to reduce the chances that products or services will be of poor quality after the project has been completed.

QA is done not only to the products and services delivered by the project but also to the process and procedures used to manage the project, that includes the way the project uses the tools, techniques and methodologies to manage scope, schedule, budget and quality. Quality assurance also includes the project meets any legal or regulatory standards.

How will risks impact a project QUALITY?

Quality will be severely impacted because the project failed to produce the deliverables within scope, schedule, and budget.

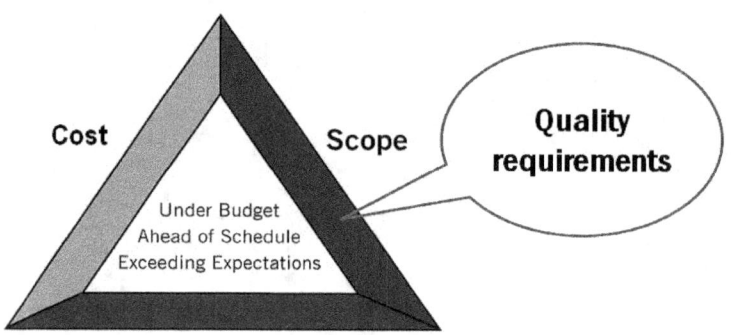

PROJECT BUDGET MUST INCLUDE A QA FUNCTION

The simple fact is that quality is an indispensable part of any effort (from both project management and system development perspectives). Building a product without quality controls is wrought with risk: it will not satisfy your customer, and will reflect poorly on your reputation. Assuming that you cannot do a change control to add a QA function to your Project Budget, the good news is that, in a pinch, you can do without a separate QA function by incorporating quality assurance into every procedure and task, and taking on quality control responsibilities yourself.

You need to incorporate rigorous review cycles into production and acceptance of every deliverable, by using peer review mechanisms as well as inviting external SME's. As is stated in the text above, "It is more important that the reviews be done than how they are done." Sometimes even having non-technical independent observers sitting in on reviews brings extra gravity and rigor to the proceedings. Another trick is getting the Customers even more closely involved in reviewing works in progress and providing feedback.

Finally, you will need to roll up your sleeves and personally check out test scripts and acceptance procedures, and join in the testing activities not necessarily to do any significant testing yourself, but to ensure that it gets done thoroughly and correctly.

WHO SHOULD BE DOING THE TESTING?

I can't trust the developers to check their own work! Can I? There are organizations where the testing function is separated into its own business unit. There are other organizations that have a separate QA function, but its members join the Project Teams at certain parts of the lifecycle, and perform testing on site. Finally, there are organizations that incorporate quality in everything they do, and thus have no separate QA function. Each approach has its own pluses and minuses, but the important concepts are:

1. Test plans and scripts need to be developed before any coding is done
2. Test scripts need to be executed faithfully, and the results communicated immediately to the developers
3. System development should not proceed until the defects have been corrected

4. The same defects in different testing cycles point to a serious problem that has to be resolved before any further work is done

QUALITY AUDIT

Quality audits are structured reviews of the quality management activities that help identify lessons learned that can improve the performance of current or future project activities. Audits are performed by project staff or consultants with expertise in specific areas. The purpose of a quality audit is to review how the project is using its internal processes to produce the products and services it will deliver to the key project stakeholders. Its goal is to find ways to improve the tools, techniques and processes that create the products and services. If problems are detected during the quality audits, corrective action will be necessary to the tools, processes and procedures used to ensure quality is re-established. Part of the audit may include a review of the project staff understanding of the quality parameters or metrics, and the skills expertise and knowledge of the people in charge of producing or delivering the products or services. If corrective actions are needed, these must be approved through the change control processes.

QUALITY MANAGEMENT VS QUALITY AUDIT

- Quality Management is all the activities that are intended to bring about the desired level of quality.

- Quality Audit is the procedural control that ensure participants are adequately following the required procedures.

- These concepts are related, but should not be confused. In particular, Quality Audit relates to the approach to quality that is laid down in quality standards such as the ISO-900x standards.

THE PDCA CYCLE

The most popular tool used to determine quality assurance is the Shewhart Cycle. This cycle for quality assurance consists of four steps: Plan, Do, Check, and Act. These steps are commonly abbreviated as PDCA.

The four quality assurance steps within the PDCA model stand for:

- **Plan:** Establish objectives and processes required to deliver the desired results.
- **Do**: Implement the process developed.
- **Check**: Monitor and evaluate the implemented process by testing the results against the predetermined objectives
- **Act**: Apply actions necessary for improvement if the results require changes.

The PDCA is an effective method for monitoring quality assurance because it analyzes existing conditions and methods used to provide the product or service to key project stakeholders. The goal is to ensure that excellence is inherent in every component of the process. Quality assurance also helps determine whether the steps used to provide the product or service is appropriate for the time and conditions. In addition, if the PDCA cycle is repeated throughout the lifetime of the project helping improve internal efficiency.

Quality assurance demands a degree of detail in order to be fully implemented at every step. Planning, for example, could include an investigation into the quality of the raw materials used in manufacturing, the actual assembly, or the inspection processes used. The Checking step could include beneficiary feedback or surveys to determine if beneficiary needs are being met or exceeded and why they are or are not. Acting could mean a total revision in the delivery process in order to correct a technical flaw.

The goal to exceed stakeholder expectations in a measurable and accountable process is provided by quality assurance.

ASSURANCE VS. CONTROL

Quality assurance is often confused with quality control; quality control is done at the end of a process or activity to verify that quality standards have been met. Quality control by itself does not provide quality, although it may identify problems and suggest ways to improve it. In contrast, quality assurance is a systematic approach to obtaining quality standards. Quality assurance is something that must be planned for from the earliest stages of a project, with appropriate measures taken at every stage. Unfortunately, far too many development projects are implemented with no quality assurance plan, and these projects often fail to meet the quality expectations of the project sponsor and key project stakeholders. To avoid problems the project must be able to demonstrate consistent compliance with the quality requirements for the project.

BUILDING REGULATIONS AND FIRE SAFETY COMPLIANCE

Performance-based fire safety provisions look at the outcomes of a successful system for fire minimization and control in a workplace or organization, without describing the detail of how this is to be achieved. For example, in Australia the *Building Code* has a series of performance requirements for the structural elements of a building, one of which is the FRL or fire-resistance level. This has up to three parts: structural adequacy; integrity; and insulation (in that order). Each is expressed in terms of minutes of required satisfactory performance; e.g. an FRL of 240/240/240 means that the structural elements would perform for four hours on all three criteria. There are performance requirements for, for example, fire doors, fire shutters and fire-stopping material (material for plugging 'penetrations' in floors, etc.). On the other hand, an example of prescriptive requirements is that for penetration of a floor, wall or ceiling by a cable or cluster of wires.

This requires penetrations to have a specified maximum cross-section. Refer also to 'Alternative methods' further on in this chapter for a note on the issue of performance versus prescription.

Legal Requirements For Fire Safety

Specific reference to fire safety is not generally included in the actual OHS act, but there will be reference to fire safety in most of the accompanying regulations. The regulations vary in adequacy.

Building Regulations And Minimum Standards Of Fire Safety

Obviously, building design alone can only be partly successful in preventing fire. Other important factors are:

- good housekeeping, separation and segregation of materials and proper storage, e.g. fire cabinets for solvents
- the transport and handling of flammable materials
- the behavior of personnel, e.g., smoking, disposal of paper, cigarettes and matches
- adhering only to uses for which the building was designed, e.g. no solvent-based printing if not designed for that
- selection of wall and floor coverings and furniture which will not spread flame from an ignition source, and will minimize the speed of travel
- extreme care with radiant heaters, and preferably use of tilt-switched radiant heaters, or wall-mounted radiant heaters
- great care with high temperature sources used in maintenance such as welding equipment

- electrical design, installation, repair and maintenance to meet national or accepted standards.

The approach to fire in buildings falls into two key areas:
- design to prevent fire
- design to limit the spread of a fire if it starts, and to limit the effects of that fire.

Before building any new buildings, an application for approval must generally be submitted to the appropriate level of government. Fire design of buildings is based on the observed characteristics of fires, some of which have been carefully reproduced in places such as the UK Fire Research Station. These characteristics are:

- in most cases the fire will only develop if there is fuel above the initial ignition source
- combustible materials in the path of the flames increase the size and intensity of the fire
- hot gases and flames, as they are lighter than air, travel upwards
- fire tends to follow vertical paths of travel – i.e. chimneys, flues, stairways, and the interior of stud walls – but drafts or forced airflows, e.g. in underground mines, can change this characteristic
- ceilings can be a barrier to this upward spread
- sometimes the lateral and downward spread is increased by the presence of highly flammable coatings or bonding, glues, varnishes and lacquers
- the likelihood of flammable surfaces catching fire from radiant heat energy, rather than direct spread, depends to

some extent on the rate of burning of the fire in materials providing the radiant heat.

WORKPLACE FIRE SAFETY TIPS

Fires are among the biggest cause of casualties in the workplace, but being proactive and implementing a fire plan can significantly help reduce the risk. The most important thing to consider when creating a fire plan is to determine the likelihood of a fire.

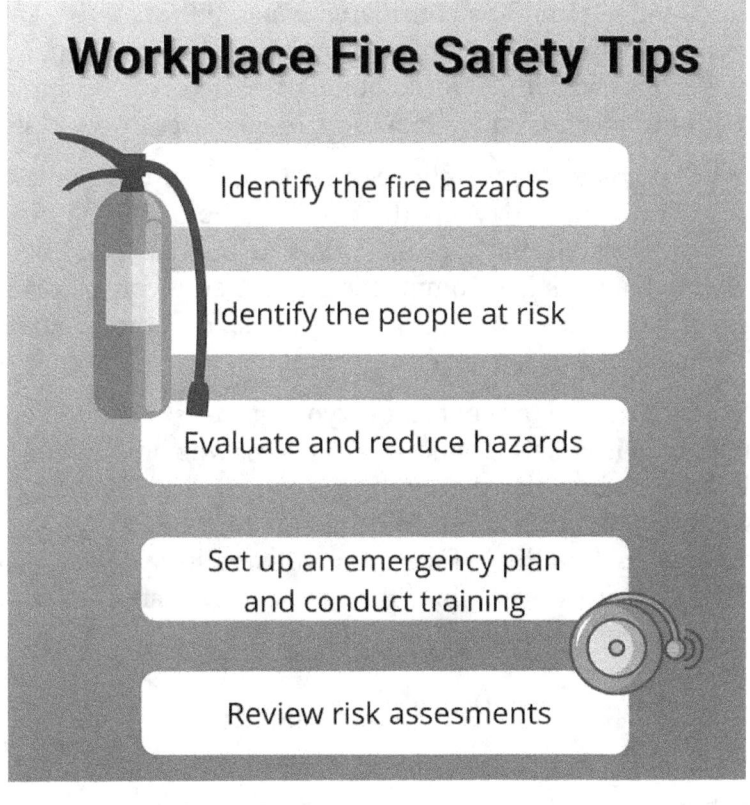

IDENTIFY THE RISKS

A fire hazard may look different in each workplace. From the fire triangle, we know that the 3 sources of fire are ignition, fuel and oxygen. Identify areas that carry the risk of ignition such as electrical equipment, boilers, hot works processes, steam pipes, and other sources of heat.

Define the classification of fuels in your workplace and the type of fire extinguisher required. Class A fuels include wood, paper, cloth, trash, plastics, or any solid combustible materials that are not metals. Class B fuels are flammable liquids like gasoline, oil, grease, acetone, or any non-metal in a liquid state, on fire. Class C fuels are energized electrical equipment so, as long as it's "plugged in," it would be considered a class C fire. Class D fuels are metals, potassium, sodium, aluminum, and magnesium. Lastly, Class K fuels are defined as a cooking fire involving combustion from liquids used in food preparation, like greases or cooking oils.

And of course, fires only need about 16% of oxygen to burn. Trying to minimize oxygen flow in fires across large areas or plants isn't feasible but for small fires, using dirt, sand, or non-flammable blankets is recommended. Make sure you are aware of any ventilation, air conditioning systems, or other sources of airflow in hazard-prone areas.

If there's a fire, of course, everyone is at risk. But it's critical to know who is in and around the premises, who among your staff work alone or in isolated areas, requires extra care such as elders or workers with special needs, or is new to the facility. Keeping continuous track of this information will simplify your evacuation plan and processes in the case of an emergency.

EVALUATE AND REDUCE RISKS

Removing fire hazards in the workplace is easier said than done, but preventative action can be taken. Make sure not to use any damaged electrical cords or tools and to not overload circuits.

Equipment maintenance and safe chemical usage and storage are also important factors in preventing fire hazards. Keeping your work area clean from dust and debris may sound like basic housekeeping, but as we can see from the Imperial Sugar Company dust explosion, keeping dust from building up in the workplace can be a matter of life and death.

Use PPE when in contact with fire hazards such as but not limited to flame-resistant gloves, jackets, and pants. OSHA states that if fire hazards are present, or likely to be present in the workplace the employer will have each affected employee use the types of PPE that will protect the affected employee from the hazards identified in the hazard assessment.

So, what does an emergency plan look like?

- Have a preferred method for reporting fires and other emergencies.
- Make sure evacuation policy and procedures are in place.
- Determine route assignments, such as floor plans, workplace maps, and safe or refuge areas.
- Keep all names, titles, departments, and telephone numbers of individuals both within and outside your company to contact for additional information or explanation of duties and responsibilities under the emergency plan;
- Create procedures for employees who remain to shut down or perform critical plant operations, operate fire extinguishers, or perform other essential services that cannot be shut down for every emergency alarm before evacuating; and
- Establish rescue and medical duties for any workers designated to perform them.

If your workplace is required to have an emergency plan, the employer is then required to provide the necessary training regarding workplace fire safety. Basic training for employers, employees, management, or engineers includes hazard communication, handling of materials, fire detection and prevention requirements, fire extinguishers, and more. Conducting periodic evacuation drills and fire extinguisher inspections can also help reinforce the steps and actions that need to be taken across your workforce.

BUILDING COMPLIANCE WITH FIRE SAFETY REGULATIONS

Building codes may include:

- fire-resisting construction
- compartmentation and separation
- protection of openings
- structural tests for lightweight construction
- early fire hazard indices
- fire doors, smoke doors, fire windows and shutters
- penetrations
- emergency lighting, exit signs and warning systems
- smoke hazard management
- fire-fighting equipment, and when sprinklers are required
- lift installations
- fire isolated exits
- number of exits
- distances to exits and second exits.

Fire-Resisting Construction

This includes constructing a building to protect it from fire in another, and using materials which minimize the spread of fire and generation of smoke and toxic gases. 'Stability' must be enough to allow escape and firefighter safety, and to minimize collapse onto nearby property. Standard fire tests are used to decide if different parts of a building will perform satisfactorily. 'Structural adequacy' looks at the ability of a structural part to continue to support a load. The 'integrity' aspect looks at how well a structural member prevents fire, gases and flames getting through it. Insulation is designed to limit heat transmission so that something on the other side of a wall or floor does not receive enough heat flow to ignite.

Compartmentation And Separation

Compartmentation refers to the division of a building into 'compartments' separated by structural material of specified fire resistance, such as a fire wall, to prevent spread of fire and smoke, and facilitate access by firefighters. 'Separation' limits the opportunity for the fire to spread to other buildings. (There was recently a fatal blaze in a park home (semiportable home) which threatened to ignite others nearby.) It also refers to separation of certain key equipment such as sprinkler valve equipment. Separation for dangerous goods also separates the goods from fire sources such as roadways.

Protection Of Openings

Certain types and layouts of doorways, windows, infill panels and fixed or openable glazed areas may be covered by a building code. It may include, for example, distances between windows on either side of a fire wall, and where protection of the opening is required, internal or external wall-wetting sprinklers, or automatic fire doors for doorways, automatic fire shutters for windows or construction of approved FRL for other openings.

STRUCTURAL TESTS FOR LIGHTWEIGHT CONSTRUCTION

These may cover the requirements for materials such as sheet or board, plaster, sprayed insulation, and concrete mixed with soft products such as pumice, which can be damaged by impact, pressure or abrasion, and thinner forms of masonry.

EARLY FIRE HAZARD INDICES

These deal with materials, linings and surface finishes in buildings, particularly fire-isolated exits. Three indices are used flammability, spread-of-flame and smoke developed, which are measured by standard tests. In addition, protection of sides and edges from exposure to air may be a requirement.

FIRE DOORS, SMOKE DOORS, FIRE WINDOWS AND SHUTTERS

Fire doors are required to meet certain specifications and glazed parts must meet the integrity requirement in the FRL. Smoke doors must of course prevent smoke passing and, if glazed, minimize the risk of injury if a person accidentally walks into them.

PENETRATIONS

Penetrations refer to services which penetrate walls, floors and ceilings required to have a FRL. Metal and UPVC pipes, wires and cables, electrical switches and outlets, and the fire-stopping material are all considered.

Emergency Lighting, Exit Signs, And Warning Systems

This part of a building code may cover the requirements for provision and design of lighting and emergency signage which will retain illumination in occupied areas and in egress ways, such as fire-isolated stairways, ramps or passageways independent of the normal power supply.

Smoke Hazard Management

Various classifications of buildings may be required by a code to have smoke control systems. This includes particular requirements such as natural smoke venting, smoke exhaust systems, air handling systems of a particular design, and smoke doors. In particular, smoke must be excluded from fire-isolated exits.

Lift Installations

A number of issues arise with lifts. These include restrictions on use in a fire, fitting out as an emergency lift for mobility-challenged people and fire service personnel, and prevention of spread-of-fire by way of lift shafts and doors.

Fire-Isolated Exits

Fire-isolated exits, and the provision for reaching them via fire-isolated stairways and ramps, are important features in some buildings.

Distances To Exits And Second Exits

The distance to an exit is clearly an important issue. Requirements vary with the class of building.

FIRE-FIGHTING EQUIPMENT AND WHEN SPRINKLERS ARE REQUIRED

Fire-fighting equipment includes fire hydrants, hose reels, sprinklers and fire control centers. Special care is needed in a building being constructed, in which sources of ignition may be more likely and fire systems are yet to be installed.

FIRE EXTINGUISHERS

While many fire authorities require the installation of fire extinguishers in laboratories, the CHO should understand that, because of the relatively high nozzle pressure of extinguishers, the stream of the released extinguishing materials may sweep many breakable chemical containers off laboratory benches or cabinets and thereby contribute to explosive and flammable risk, as well as to the risk of toxic fumes generated either through heat or the reactivity of mixed chemicals. Extinguishers should be used in the laboratory only by authorized personnel who have received appropriate training, which should include actual practice. In the absence of an ongoing commitment to such training, the CHO is advised that it is best to focus on laboratory evacuation and to restrict the use of extinguishers to fight so-called "basket-fires" (i.e., fires that can easily be extinguished with minimal involvement of the overall laboratory space). Of course, the selection of extinguishing materials, including those contained in portable extinguishers or in any automatic fire suppressant system, must be guided by the reactivity (e.g., water reactivity) of laboratory chemicals, and should be undertaken only in strict coordination with fire science professionals.

Design Features Of A Building Affecting Structural Integrity

Type of construction

As mentioned earlier the particular method of construction of a building, and its layout, affect its structural integrity in a fire. For a building of multiple classification, the most fire-resisting type of construction may be required, applying the most classification for a single-storey to all storey, with perhaps certain exceptions. Sports spectator venues need special attention. A soccer ground fire at the Bradford Football Stadium in the United Kingdom in 1985 indicates how important this is.

Compartmentation and Separation

Compartmentation and separation affect the spread of fire and smoke, and codes may cover maximum sizes of fire compartments and atria. Atria (atriums) in buildings potentially could allow easy travel of fire and smoke from level to level.

Vertical Separation and Fire Walls

Vertical separation of openings such as windows is generally covered in codes, and fire walls which create compartment. (In a recent two-storey school fire, the fire spread rapidly along the ceiling because fire walls did not break up the ceiling space.)

Lift (Elevator) Shafts, Sprinkler Valves and Openings

Lift shafts could easily transmit fire and smoke and these are covered in codes. Certain equipment such as sprinkler valves must be fire-isolated. Openings in external walls and fire walls require protection.

Services and penetrations

Services passing through a floor are covered by codes. Penetrations of floors, walls or ceilings between compartments for cables, etc., have a limit on size and must be fire-stopped, e.g. caulked with suitable material. Materials, linings and surface finishes are covered, and may deal with what are called 'early fire hazard indices', EFHIs.

SPRINKLERS

Codes generally set out sprinkler requirements.

METHODS OF IMPROVING FIRE SAFETY OF BUILDINGS

'Passive protection' refers to protecting a building by attempting to confine a fire to the area in which it started. Automatic venting or blocking of the products of combustion is involved.

Passive protection includes:

- fire-retarding treatments and material
- air conditioning which can switch to fire mode, i.e. no return air recycling
- stairway, passageway and lift shaft pressurization if a fire occurs
- the correct fire rating of all walls, roofs, doors, floors, ceilings, windows and structural members
- fire doors, fire windows and fire shutters.

Smoke and heat management is important to allow occupants to escape and to reduce the temperature build-up. 'Active protection' is aimed at detecting and extinguishing a fire once it has started. It includes:

- fire and smoke detectors and alarms

- fire hydrants, hose reels and extinguishers, including water pressure booster pumps
- automatic sprinkler systems
- gas flooding systems
- evacuation systems.

The detection system can be wired to a fire panel and also linked to the fire services.

REQUIREMENTS FOR EGRESS FROM A BUILDING

Building codes cover access and egress, and emergency lighting, exit signs and warning systems. It may involve fire-isolated passageways, ramps and stairways. An 'exit' has a wide range of meanings; generally, it takes the form of an internal or external stairway, a doorway opening to a street or open space, a fire-isolated passageway or a doorway situated within a fire wall. The door has to open in the direction of travel to the outside. The best building design in the world is no use if the exit is locked or blocked with goods. Exit doors must be readily openable while the building is occupied. Exit doors must not be chained, bolted, fastened, or obstructed in any way. They should be openable by a single-handed action from the inside by a single device. They must not be blocked by traffic or parked vehicles on the outside. Special attention is required for invalids, people in bed due to illness, elderly people, people whose movement is impaired, very young children, and people in captivity.

BUILDING DESIGN, EMERGENCY PROCEDURES AND HUMAN BEHAVIOR

In situations where people have died in a fire, generally it is smoke and toxic gas inhalation which kills or renders people unconscious so they cannot escape rather than heat itself. While it is necessary to sound an alarm and alert people so that they respond ('Fire!'), there is the risk that panic can arise. This is more likely if there is a delay in giving a warning, and hence time is short to evacuate a large number of people. If exits to the outside are blocked or have been locked, and a crush develops, people can panic further. In some cases, such as the Bradford soccer stadium fire in the UK, many people died from crushing, not from fire. (Multiple deaths also resulted from exits with illegal locking or from inadequate egress in the Whisky A Go Go nightclub fire in Brisbane, the Stardust nightclub fire in Dublin and a more recent nightclub fire in Shanghai.) A prompt and clear response by well-trained staff will ensure that panic is minimized and evacuation is effective. It is important that physically challenged people are properly briefed in advance, because if they set off down an emergency stair at the wrong time they can obstruct the exit of many others. Problems can arise in buildings where large numbers of people inside are casual visitors, such as in major shopping centers. Tenants may change and appointment of new wardens overlooked. Exit routes should be well marked and signposting good. Panic can cause people to overlook obvious escape routes, and can lead to individual competitive responses rather than orderly behavior where members of a group look after each other.

BENCHMARKING FACILITIES COSTS

In facilities management, benchmarking has been defined as 'a process of comparing a product, service process, indeed, any activity or object, with other samples from a peer group, with a view to identifying 'best buy' or 'best practice' and targeting oneself to emulate it'.3 This definition effectively outlines one of the most important (but often misunderstood) aspects concerning facilities management benchmarking, that is, 'targeting' or taking action in order to release value to the organization. Facilities managers should fully understand the reasons why they are embarking on a benchmarking exercise; they are often forced into following a market trend, an organizational mandate, or the potentially dangerous misbelief that at the end of the exercise costs can be cut. Of course, benchmarking is about saving costs, where possible, but it is also about performance and value, and fundamentally, customer requirements.

The need for benchmarking within organizations can also be linked directly to the competitive environment in which they operate. Globalization and information and communications technology advances inevitably mean that organizations must be increasingly dynamic in order to stave off the competition. Over the past 20 years there has been a business performance revolution which has been characterized by the introduction of methodologies and techniques such as activity-based costing, the balanced scorecard, the business excellence model, the performance pyramid and shareholder value frameworks, all of which are approaches that many facilities managers will have experienced or even feared.

The techniques discussed above are useful when talking about the value chain that exists within organizations where the facilities management department or its activities could be described as a critical link. The techniques ultimately provide strategic management information through the use of performance measures (in various proportions and mixes) associated with the following issues/themes:

- stakeholders' (e.g. investors/shareholders, regulators, suppliers, employees)
- satisfaction/contribution
- leadership (e.g. experience, skill)
- company policies and strategies
- processes, skills, policies and procedures (e.g. time, quality, safety, waste efficiency)
- cost drivers (e.g. resource, productivity, supply chain)

- financial (e.g. cost of capital, share earnings, profitability, operating costs)
- capabilities (e.g. technology absorption)
- innovation and learning (e.g. training and development)
- customer satisfaction, loyalty and profitability.

MISINTERPRETING THE VALUE OF BENCHMARKING

It is common for benchmarking to be incorrectly mixed up with performance measurement techniques. The truth, however, is that benchmarking is a systematic process of evaluation; it should be a fluid methodology that uses performance criteria (among other measurements) in the search for improvement beyond best practice. Within the facilities management discipline this misconception is prevalent, largely as a result of facilities managers often viewing occupancy costs as their only output, rather than taking the wider view of adding value to the organization by providing support through accommodation, workplaces and services. In addition, facilities managers always try to rely on general indicators that are typically available in the public domain. Those who understand the nature of facilities management service provision will readily understand that this comparison provides no value at all, since different cost levels are driven by individual building/location characteristics and the quality-of-service provision.

The wider perspective Facilities managers need to add value to the organizational value chain. There needs to be a realization that the discipline of facilities management encompasses much more than cost alone. True facilities management benchmarking activities can be largely associated with evaluation of the following aspects:

- assets

- inputs
- processes
- outputs
- systems

Buildings are significant assets to many organizations and the facilities manager would typically be concerned with such issues as physical, functional and financial performance. In this respect there are many methods of evaluating asset performance and feeding information into the benchmarking process. For example, building condition, post-occupancy evaluation, building quality assessment and investment appraisal techniques are all capable of providing data for comparative evaluation. Furthermore, the relatively simple analysis of space utilization is often overlooked, although this in fact influences many of the other issues listed above.

Inputs can be associated with processes and outputs and can relate to many different circumstances within the remit of a facilities manager. For example, the procurement of a new building would be a discrete project with inputs and various activities interacting to make identifiable processes, the final output being the asset or building. The principal inputs in this case would be the labor and materials being used throughout the construction process. The provision of a catering service would normally depend on various inputs such as catering staff labor and raw food ingredients, the outputs being meals, and so on. Possible measures that a facilities manager may wish to use during the course of input/process/output benchmarking could relate to (examples given are as applied to security service provision):

- cost (e.g. hourly cost of guarding, cost of surveillance activities, total cost of security per annum)
- quality (e.g. employee skill/experience level, accuracy of intelligence reports, number of shoplifters apprehended or customer satisfaction)

- time (e.g. surveillance hours per annum, time taken to assimilate intelligence information, time to apprehend thieves)
- risk (e.g. health and safety breach by security staff, injury to third parties due to an unplanned activity, excessive loss to the business through theft)

Systems refer to the mechanisms that are in place to assist with the efficiency of processes. In the case of a new building project an example might be a web-based information system for sharing project knowledge. In relation to facilities management service delivery activities a computer-aided facilities management (CAFM) system should collect information to assist with the management of processes. Measurements relating to time, cost, quality and risk may equally be applicable in the case of systems.

The facilities audit represents a review of the costs of providing office space and services within an organization. It is important to realize that the audit is not concerned with cost alone, but also includes analysis of the building and organizational characteristics that drive cost (resource drivers) and the associated levels of performance.

RESOURCE DRIVERS

A resource driver is a characteristic that influences the required levels and/or deployment of a resource. It is important for the facilities manager to understand that output performance (for example, how clean a building is) may remain at the same level even though the level of resource required (for example, the number of cleaners and frequency of cleaning operations) varies in different buildings (an otherwise comparable building may, for example, be located beside an area of pollution which increases the amount of dirt accumulating on the glazing).

Resource drivers have been classified as:

- quantitative: usually relating to characteristics of the building or organization that can be readily measured, for example, floor area, window area, number of staff and contractors' staff, number of covers served in a restaurant
- qualitative: characteristics such as the location of the building or the specific preferences or aspirations of the organization
- economic, for example, interest rates and market conditions
- operating conditions, for example, specific lease conditions and organizational aspirations.

PERFORMANCE DATA

Performance characteristics are important within benchmarking in order to identify the level of output associated with cost. Unfortunately, many organizations do not record sufficient performance-related information (although this is changing in the advent of developments in CAFM and helpdesk software), and in any case it is difficult to make comparisons between organizations which measure performance metrics differently or not at all. In such cases the facilities manager has the difficult and subjective job of comparing and measuring performance. Customer satisfaction surveys can provide a quick means of procuring performance data.

COST DATA

The retrieval of cost data will be a relatively simple process for the facilities manager who has developed and maintained facilities service budgets at a detailed level It is recommended that facilities costs are audited or collected at the greatest level of detail possible. This will ensure that the facilities manager understands what is included within an overall service cost. For example, from an accountancy point of view, a stationery budget may include reprographics supplies, whereas for the purpose of facilities management benchmarking it is often accounted for under the reprographics cost center. It is often a lack of such understanding that leads to the failure of many commercial benchmarking groups or partnerships.

PARAMETERS

Parameters are the metrics that are used to express benchmarked costs in a meaningful way. In order to provide useful statistics, it is necessary to establish a direct relationship between the parameter and the cost of service. For example, it is unlikely that vending costs can be related to floor space, whereas there will, under normal circumstances, be a directly proportional relationship with the number of staff or occupants using the building in a 24-hour period. Similarly, it is common to express the costs associated with premises services on a cost per square meter of floor area, and support services such as catering, mail distribution and stationery are commonly expressed as costs per capita.

Parameters must be measured on a comparable basis between the organization and its peer group. The RICS Code of Measurement Practice provides a standard protocol for floor space measurements that has been readily adopted within the industry. It should be noted that it is common for different countries to have slight deviations from this standard. Comparing facilities costs using incorrect and incompatible parameters renders the benchmarking process ineffective. Services maintenance costs can be seen to vary significantly (in benchmarking terms) because of the use of GIA and NIA; it is a common error for facilities managers to use the wrong parameter by mistake. All too often, professional and managerial reports relating to premises and facilities are littered with incorrectly described floor area measurements. This is also a common reason for commercial benchmarking partnerships failing.

Chapter 3 : COST MANAGEMENT

Whether you are developing a new product, designing a facility, or changing a key process, it's challenging to forecast and manage project costs effectively. In fact, the job is so challenging that half of all large IT projects massively blow their budgets, running on average 45 percent over budget and seven percent over time, according to consultants McKinsey & Co. For projects in other sectors, the news is no better. The American Academy of Project Management reported that companies were completing only 50 percent of projects within their original budget. However, strong cost management helps you avoid that fate.

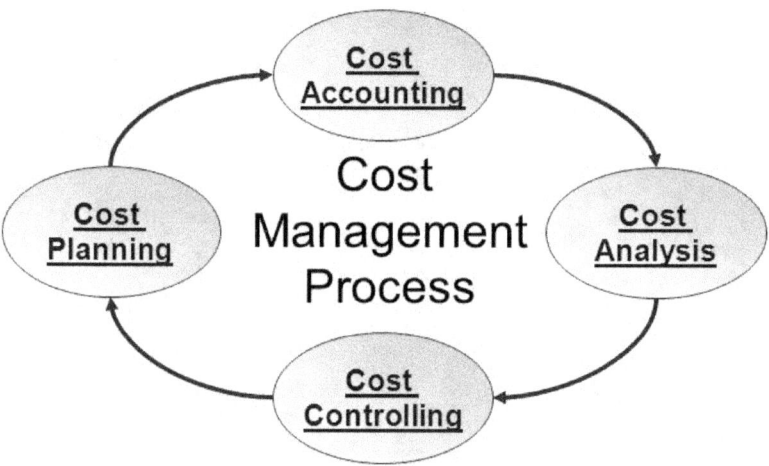

Cost management refers to the activities concerning planning and controlling a project's budget. Effective cost management ensures that a project is completed on budget and according to its planned scope. Since you assess the success of a project at least in part by its cost performance, cost management is a prime determinant of the project outcome. Cost management activities are conducted throughout the project life cycle, from planning and budget allocation to controlling costs during project execution and assessing a project's cost performance upon completion. Although cost management includes a whole ensemble of activities, it is sometimes referred to in terms of more specific functions, such as spend management, cost accounting, and cost transparency. Cost managers sometimes use these terms as loose synonyms for the broad cost management function. Cost Management is comprised of four primary processes: Resource Planning, Cost Estimating, Cost Budgeting, and Cost Control.

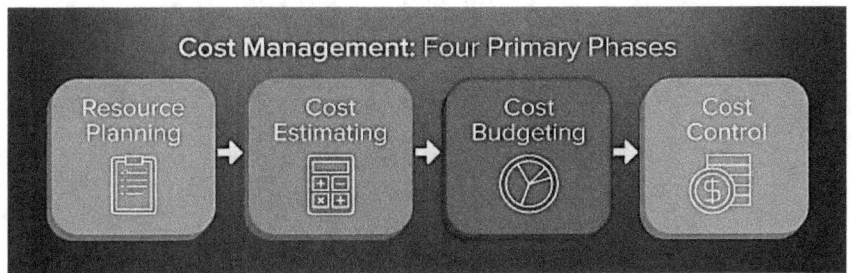

Resource Planning

Part of the initiation stage of a project, the resource planning process uses a work breakdown structure which is a hierarchical representation of all project deliverables and the work required to complete them. This process will determine the full cost of resources needed to complete a project successfully. Managers typically determine the required resources for each work breakdown structure component and then add them to create a total resource cost estimate for all project deliverables.

Cost Estimating

Cost estimating is an iterative process that uses a variety of estimating techniques to determine the total cost of completing a project. Cost estimating techniques vary widely in their approaches to computing project costs and stretch from conceptual techniques that draw mainly from historical experience and expert judgment to determinative techniques that estimate costs on a component-by-component basis. We will discuss these techniques in detail later, as they vary in their levels of accuracy. Determinative techniques are the most accurate; however, while the estimator's job is always to create the most accurate estimate possible, determinative estimating techniques are only an option if you've reasonably finalized a project's scope and deliverables. As such, you use the less accurate estimating techniques during the earliest stages of project planning, and then revise and update estimates as the project continues to be defined.

COST BUDGETING

Once you have created satisfactory estimates, you can finalize and approve the project's budget. Cost managers typically release budgeted amounts in stages according to the level of a project's progress. These allocations include contingencies and reserves.

COST CONTROL

Cost control is the practice of measuring a project's cost performance according to cost and schedule baselines that provide points of comparison throughout the project life cycle. The specific requirements for effective cost control are set out in the project management plan. The individual in charge of cost management investigates the reasons for cost variations if they deem cost variations unacceptable, corrective action will be initiated. Cost control also includes other related responsibilities, such as ensuring that updated project budgets reflect changes to a project's scope.

Cost management involves Scope Management, Time Management, Quality Management, Risk Management, and Human Resource Management. An engineering manager needs to work closely with the Project Manager to provide input into the cost associated with delivering the project, changes affecting the scope of the project, risks and contingencies that will impact the project implementation, resources required to deliver the project, the penalty to be incurred should the project timeline is extended, et cetera.

PROJECT COST MANAGEMENT PLAN

The project cost management plan guides these four processes. Created during the project planning phase, the cost management plan is a document that defines how you manage, control, and communicate a project's costs in order to complete the project on budget. Among other things, a cost management plan identifies the individual or group responsible for cost management, details how you will assess a project's cost performance, and sets rules for how to communicate cost performance to project shareholders. It also establishes the methodologies by which you will control project cost variations.

While you can customize a cost management plan to fit your organization's needs, they generally follow a standard format. Sections often include the cost variance plan, the cost management approach, information on cost estimation, the cost baseline, cost control, and reporting processes, the change control process, the project budget, and approvals. You may also want to include the spending authority levels for key project personnel, specifying which roles can approve costs up to specific thresholds.

Cost Variance Plan

Cost variance is when the actual amount differs from the budgeted amount. In your cost management plan, you'll need a section that details the actions you should take, including who is held responsible in the case of cost variance. The size of the variance usually necessitates different actions: a cost variance of less than five percent might result in an explanation of that variance, while a 95 percent or greater variance could force the project to be abandoned.

Cost Management Approach

This section outlines the approach a manager uses for cost management. The level of rigor can vary, but this describes how to establish a cost baseline and how to compare actual costs. You usually track and report costs through control accounts, where you roll up the costs of subtasks. This often occurs at the third level of the work breakdown structure, a tool that breaks a project into small components or chunks of work to determine the resources needed to complete a job or project. However, the point at which you track and report depends on the scope of the project.

Cost Estimation

Here you will define the methods used for estimating project costs, the levels of variation, and the expected precision, accuracy, and risk.

Cost Baseline

This has a specialized meaning in project management and represents the authorized, time-phased spending plan against which you measure cost performance. It's the sum of the estimated project cost and contingency reserves.

KEY COMPONENTS OF A COST ESTIMATE

A cost estimate is a summation of all the costs involved in successfully finishing a project, from inception to completion. These project costs can be categorized in a number of ways and levels of detail, but the simplest classification divides costs into two main categories: direct costs and indirect costs.

Direct costs

Direct costs are broadly classified as those directly associated with a single area (such as a department or a project). In project management, direct costs are expenses billed exclusively to a specific project. They can include project team wages, the costs of resources to produce physical products, fuel for equipment, and money spent to address any project-specific risks.

Indirect costs

Indirect costs, on the other hand, cannot be associated with a specific cost center and are instead incurred by a number of projects simultaneously, sometimes in varying amounts. In project management, quality control, security costs, and utilities are usually classified as indirect costs since they are shared across a number of projects and are not directly billable to any one project.

A cost estimate is more than a simple list of costs, however: it also outlines the assumptions underlying each cost. These assumptions (along with estimates of cost accuracy) are compiled into a report called the basis of estimate, which also details cost exclusions and inclusions. The basis of the estimate report allows project stakeholders to interpret project costs and to understand how and where actual costs might differ from approximated costs.

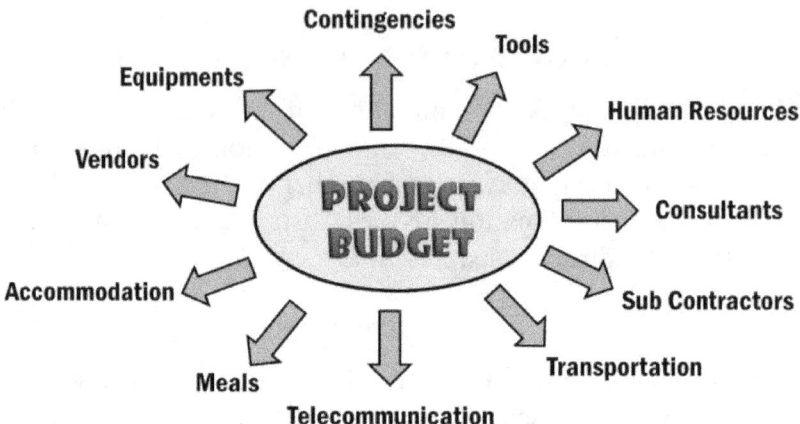

Beyond the broad classifications of direct and indirect costs, project expenses fall into more specific categories. Common types of expenses include:

- **Labor:** The cost of human effort expended towards project objectives.
- **Materials:** The cost of resources needed to create products.
- **Equipment:** The cost of buying and maintaining equipment used in project work.
- **Services:** The cost of external work that a company seeks for any given project (vendors, contractors, etc.).
- **Software:** Non-physical computer resources.
- **Hardware:** Physical computer resources.
- **Facilities:** The cost of renting or using specialized equipment, services, or locations.

- **Contingency costs:** Costs added to the project budget to address specific risks.

CREATE PROJECT ESTIMATES AT CRITICAL POINTS

Cost estimates are critical to successful project management, so teams are expected to produce a reasonably accurate and reliable estimate during the conception and definition phase of a project. Estimates are adjusted for accuracy during the planning phase, as project stakeholders and sponsors may ask for revisions before they are willing to authorize a budget. After this early stage, the accuracy of estimates is systematically increased.

Cost estimating is an ongoing process, and estimate revisions are normal in order to ensure accuracy throughout project execution. Typically, work scheduled in the near future will have the most accurate estimates, while work scheduled farther away in time have less accurate estimates. This approach is known as rolling wave planning.

Detailed cost estimates are usually broken down into greater levels of detail and supplementary information. These outputs typically include:

- Activity cost estimates for the activities that make up a project.
- Supporting details, which include assumptions underlying estimates, cost data sources, and cost element sensitivity.
- Requested changes, which a newer, more accurate cost estimate may prompt.
- Updates to the cost management plan, such as those necessitated by changes to the project scope.
- Inputs for subsequent planning processes that use cost estimates.

Direct Costs

Direct costs are those which you can directly associate with a specific cost object. They are billable for specific projects.

Indirect Costs

You cannot associate indirect costs with a specific cost object, and you typically incur indirect costs by a number of projects at the same time. They are not billable to specific projects.

Fixed Costs

Fixed costs are costs you incur during manufacturing that are not associated with the volume of produced output.

Variable Costs

Variable costs are costs you incur during manufacturing that are directly associated with the volume of produced output.

Sunk Cost

A sunk cost is an expense you cannot recoup once it is incurred.

Opportunity Cost

When selecting a course of action, its opportunity cost is the loss of potential benefits from all alternative courses of action.

To create accurate estimates, cost estimators use a combination of estimating techniques that allow for varying levels of accuracy. While the cost estimator always aims to create the most accurate estimate possible, they may have to start with less accurate estimates and revise once the project scope and deliverables are fleshed out. The most widely used cost-estimating techniques are:

Analogous estimating

Like expert judgment, analogous estimating also called top-down estimating or historical costing relies on historical project data to form estimates for new projects. Analogous estimating draws from a purpose-built archive of historical project data, often specific to an organization. If an organization repeatedly performs similar projects, it becomes easier to draw parallels between project deliverables and their associated costs, and to adjust these according to the scale and complexity of a project.

Analogous estimating can be quite accurate if used to form estimates for similar projects and if experts can precisely assess the factors affecting costs. For example, a similar project conducted three years ago might be used as the basis for a new project cost estimate. Adjust the estimate upward for inflation, downward for the number of resources required, and upward again for the project's level of difficulty. These adjustments are typically stated as percentage changes. A new project might require 10 percent more preparation time and 15 percent more resources.

Bottom-up estimating

Also called analytical estimating, this is the most accurate estimating technique - if a complete work breakdown structure is available. A work breakdown structure decomposes project deliverables into a series of work packages (each work package comprised of a series of tasks). The project team estimates the cost of completing each task and eventually creates a cost estimate for the entire project by summing up the costs of all its constituent tasks and work packages, hence the name bottom-up. Bottom-up estimates can draw from the knowledge of experienced project teams, who are better equipped to provide task cost estimates.

While deterministic estimating techniques such as bottom-up estimating are undoubtedly the most accurate, they can also be time-consuming, especially in large and complex projects with numerous work breakdown structure components. It is not unusual for definitive estimates to also use techniques such as stochastic, parametric, and expert-judgment-based estimating (if these have proved suitably accurate in early estimates). That said, bottom-up estimating is also the most versatile estimating technique and you can use it for many types of projects.

Parametric estimating

For projects that involve similar tasks with high degrees of repeatability, use a parametric estimating technique to create highly accurate estimates using unit costs. To use parametric estimating, first divide a project into units of work. Then, you must determine the cost per unit, and then multiply the number of units by the cost per unit to estimate the total cost. These units might be the length in feet of pipeline to be laid, or the area in square yards of the ceiling to be painted. As long as the cost per unit is accurate, estimators determine quite precise and accurate estimates.

The first step towards robust cost management is having a clear idea of your project's likely costs. However, it's futile to track and control costs if you base your spending on unrealistic estimates. Project estimating considers several variables, including the method you use to create the estimate, the stage at which you build your estimate, and the types of costs you include. The first variable is the method you employ. You can produce cost estimates using a variety of estimating techniques, depending on the extent to which you define a project and the type of information you have access to. Here are some common estimation techniques:

Estimating - Methods

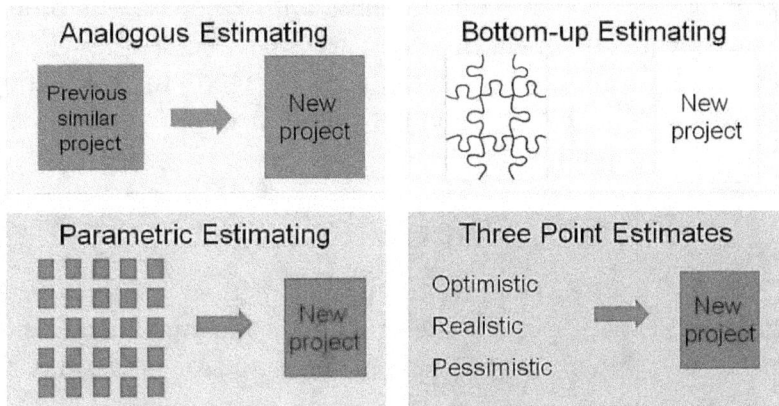

ANALOGOUS ESTIMATING

This uses historical data from similar past projects to create estimates for new projects. This method works if you have experience with projects of the same type.

PARAMETRIC ESTIMATING

This method estimates time and cost by multiplying per unit or per task amounts by the total number expected in the project. The rates are often standard or publicly published rates and can be expressed in hours of work, the amount of data entered, or the number of units of a product manufactured. This technique has a reputation for good reliability, but it's less relevant when the output isn't uniform, such as when writing computer code. Some projects have widely varied or unprecedented tasks, so they do not lend themselves to this method.

Bottom-Up Estimating

This is a determinative estimating technique that estimates costs for work breakdown structure components and adds them together to create a cost estimate for an entire project. The project team members help create the estimate. Since the people who are going to be doing the work are engaged in estimating, professionals consider this method highly accurate, as well as a team commitment builder.

Three-Point Estimating

This is a PERT-related statistical method that uses the optimistic (lowest), pessimistic (highest), and most likely cost estimates to create expected values and standard deviations for project expenditures.

Software-Based Estimating

You can use software-based estimating techniques, such as Monte Carlo simulation, to model the effects of risk events on project costs. Another factor influencing the cost estimating is the stage at which you build your cost estimate. As a project progresses, you discover more variables and actual costs, so project estimates become more refined. You can classify cost estimates based on how well you define the project scope at the time of estimation and on the type of estimation technique you use, the latter generally determines the accuracy of an estimate.

Cost Control and Reporting Process

This section establishes how you measure costs and their key metrics during the project.

Change Control Process

This describes the process for making changes to the cost baseline and how to approve those proposed changes.

Project Budget

The budget builds on the cost baseline by totaling the cost of executing the project (including contingencies for possible risks). It also adds in management reserves, which is an amount to cover unanticipated risks or unidentified events that may arise. An organization will usually set a policy for this, and the amount is often five to 15 percent of the total budget.

Cost Control

Cost Control is the task of overseeing and managing project expenses as well as preparing for potential financial risks. This job is typically the project manager's responsibility with the assistance of a cost engineer. Cost control involves not only managing the budget, but also planning, and preparing for potential risks. During the implementation and execution of projects, procedures for control and record-keeping are very important to project managers. In project management, the tool serves a different purpose in recording different financial transactions to indicate the problems or progress that are associated with the project.

Control costs are defined as processes for monitoring the status of a project in order to update the project costs. This will allow project managers to manage the changes in the cost baseline if present. It is important to take note that there will be changes in the cost in any project life cycle. The benefit of the control costs is that it gives project managers a way to determine different variances from the plan, particularly on the cost so that they can take the appropriate corrective action to reduce the risk.

Project management relies on control costs in order to determine the changes in the costs involved in implementing and executing the project. It relies on both inputs and outputs in order to analyze the cost data. The inputs necessary include the project management plan, funding requirements, work performance data and organizational structure. Using this information, project managers can create different outputs such as cost forecasts, change requests, project management plan updates and other updates concerning the documents and organizational structure.

Control costs require project managers to constantly review the budget as well as other financial information on a regular basis. This will ensure that all costs will be accounted for as well as determine the potential cost risk of the project. Simply coming up with a project budget is not enough during the planning session of your project. It is crucial for the entire team to keep a watchful eye on the cost to be always aware of the risks and how to avoid or mitigate them.

A costing technique is a way in which you compute the total cost of producing a product or performing a task. Depending on the activity or activities being costed, you may use a variety of techniques.

Job Costing

Managers use job costing, also called job-order costing, to determine the cost of a product that is unique or dissimilar to other products. In industries such as construction, it's extremely rare for two jobs to be identical. Job-order costing uses a unique job-cost record that compiles total labor and resource costs, as well as applicable overheads, for each task or activity completed as part of a task to determine total expenditures for the job. The job-cost record includes both direct and indirect costs.

Process Costing

You use process costing to determine costs for products or tasks that are identical. Unlike job costing, it does not compute the total cost of a product by summing up the costs of all tasks and activities that go into creating the product. Instead, process costing looks at the processes included in the mass production that creates products. By dividing the total cost of a process by the number of units output, it is possible to determine the cost per unit of each process. After this, you may total the costs per unit of every process involved in the eventual manufacturing of the product. In this way, you compute the cost per unit of each product on a process-by-process basis.

ACTIVITY-BASED COSTING

Activity-based costing (ABC) is an approach to assigning overhead costs to products. Since overhead cost allocation based simply on the number of machine hours needed may be misleading, this costing technique looks at the activities focused on creating a product, testing, machine setup, etc. and then assigns portions of their costs to all products created using these activities. Products that were not created via these activities do not have shares of these activities' costs added on.

DIRECT COSTING

Direct costing, also called contribution costing or variable costing, is a technique that only assigns variable manufacturing costs to the cost of a product. You do not add fixed manufacturing costs to the cost of creating a product but instead, associate those costs with the time period during which you incur them.

LIFE-CYCLE COSTING

Life-cycle costing is a comparative analysis technique that involves summing the total costs incurred during the life cycles of project options in order to choose the best option. Since starting capital costs may not be an accurate representation of how much a project will eventually cost, life-cycle costing includes all costs associated with ownership including maintenance and disposal costs to enable better decision making.

Cost Management In Information Technology Projects

Cost management software simplifies and expedites project cost management activities. This can ease the burden on cost engineers and make it easier to extract insights, such as the cost performance index. IT project costs are notorious for going over budget, mainly because of development approaches that allow scope creep during the product development life cycle. There is also a tendency for IT cost estimates to be less fixed than those of hard projects in fields such as construction and engineering, where maturity in planning and estimating is higher. In Information Technology Project Management, Kathy Schwalbe suggests that the people creating cost estimates for IT projects lack experience compared to specialist cost surveyors who create cost estimates for construction projects.

Furthermore, given how multifaceted these projects tend to be and how quickly IT evolves, IT projects often suffer from the "first-time, first-use penalty," which means that it is hard to form accurate estimates when a project or project elements have not been attempted before. This makes documenting lessons learned crucial for IT projects. The U.S. research and advisory firm Gartner creates a research report for the project and portfolio management market that categorizes vendors into four categories based on their ability to understand market needs and to drive the acceptance of new technologies. These are graphed on axes labelled "completeness of vision" and "ability to execute," respectively. The "magic quadrant" is the upper right of this graph in which leaders in both areas cluster.

In producing cost estimates for information technology projects, many of the conventional cost estimation practices do not adapt well to Agile project development, given this approach's emphasis on changing project scopes. However, since the primary input in Agile processes is labor not resources and that Agile development supports fixed-time iterations, use parametric estimating techniques to create accurate cost estimates. Agile development teams divide work into manageable portions for each iteration and can thus charge fixed costs depending on the number of developers needed to complete the work scheduled for each iteration.

Even here, however, there may be difficulties. Fixed price cost estimating works well for adaptation work, which focuses mainly on amending already designed IT products. Developmental work, on the other hand, is more difficult to estimate, given that it involves product design. Because Agile methods encourage scope changes, it is difficult to pre-plan the amount of time to spend on design. Therefore, cost overruns for developmental work are quite common.

On the whole, therefore, cost estimation for IT development projects (involving both developmental and adaptation work) is best conducted as a combination of top-down and bottom-up estimating. Adaptation, which is generally well defined, can be estimated using bottom-up estimating techniques since its scope is fixed. Developmental work, which does not have a fixed scope, is better estimated using top-down techniques such as expert judgment and analogous estimating.

COST MANAGEMENT IN CONSTRUCTION PROJECTS

Construction engineers, or quantity surveyors, oversee cost estimation and cost control while maintaining a project's profitability. They are responsible for ensuring that a project remains within budget while meeting its scope, quality, and performance requirements. Though the majority of construction projects are not subject to the "first-time, first-use penalty," they are still highly complex. And as hard projects, their design, scope, and budgetary requirements must be planned before work begins. Experience and formal training are essential for quantity surveyors. The evaluation and recommendation of bids are one of the quantity surveyor's primary responsibilities, though they may be engaged in a project from inception to conclusion. In fact, quantity surveyors get their name from the bill of quantities, a cost estimate prepared by the surveyor and by which contractors' tenders are assessed.

To aid cost management for large, complex projects, quantity surveyors or project managers may use cost codes discussed earlier to set up multiple cost accounts. These accounts are an essential portion of the budget marked for specific expenses such as labor, construction materials, architectural design, etc.

Construction costs span two major cost categories: those incurred in the actual construction and development of a facility and those incurred in the operations and maintenance of the facility throughout its life cycle. The first category includes things like the cost of land, labor, equipment, and materials needed to build a facility, the cost of architectural design and engineering, and the cost of facility inspection. The second category includes maintenance and repair costs, land rent and utilities costs, and the cost of operations and employing operations staff.

One factor that looms large in cost estimation for construction projects is the need for contingencies. Since construction projects are typically large-scale and performed over extended periods of time, adequate contingency planning is vital.

CONTINGENCIES IN CONSTRUCTION PROJECTS

- Schedule adjustments, which are not unusual for such large-scale projects. Given the large costs of equipment and labor in construction projects, delays and schedule extensions can increase costs considerably.

- Changes in equipment and labor costs, which are also not uncommon in lengthy projects.

- Environmental changes, such as changes in climate — again not uncommon in lengthy projects.

- Changes in design development, which, though rare, are not unheard of. These depend on the quality of pre-execution project planning and uncontrollable circumstances such as natural events.

COST ESTIMATES FOR CONSTRUCTION PROJECTS

Cost estimates for construction projects fall into three classes:

- Design estimates: Created during project planning and design, these include a number of estimates ranging in accuracy from screening through conceptual to definitive.
- Bid estimates: This is a finalized definitive estimate used to conduct competitive bidding.
- Control estimates: Use these to measure cost performance during project execution; they are susceptible to revisions during a project.

An important aspect of cost estimation in construction projects is determining the relationship between project scale and the average cost per unit. Typically, estimators using empirical data to establish these relationships will find that there are economies or diseconomies of scale. That is, the average cost per unit changes as the scale of the project increases. Estimators seek to take advantage of economies of scale to minimize unit costs.

COST MANAGEMENT IN ENGINEERING PROJECTS

Civil engineering projects (such as for highways and bridges) sometimes have added pressure from increased public interest in their progress and especially their cost performance. This can be problematic when critics fail to appreciate the iterative nature of cost estimating and draw misleading comparisons between inaccurate preliminary estimates and control estimates. This problem is compounded by the fact that civil engineering projects typically feature large degrees of uncertainty in estimates usually due to a combination of project length, natural conditions, and, in some instances, political conditions in the region. As such, organizations such as The Institution of Engineers of Ireland suggest that preliminary estimates for civil engineering projects not be made public and that more definitive estimates clearly state project scopes and underlying assumptions.

Civil engineering projects that run over extended periods of time may also have to contend with scope changes requested by changing political administrations. In some developing countries, these projects might struggle to retain political support as governments change, and it is not uncommon for there to be problems with administrative corruption. As such, civil engineering projects place special importance on adequate risk identification, and contingency reserves for these projects tend to be generous. It is also important to undertake project planning in a way that minimizes the likelihood of future scope changes, since these can easily cause cost overruns.

Chapter 4 : LEADERSHIP MANAGEMENT

Leadership is a management approach in which leaders help set strategic goals for the organization while motivating individuals within the group to successfully carry out assignments in service to those goals. It entails directing and coordinating individuals within an organization to achieve its goals or mission. Whether you're seeking to achieve higher levels of management or leadership, or you've reached a ceiling at your workplace and are looking for the next step, organizational leadership might be the right next step for you.

Leadership jobs are impacted by the company one works for and the actual position. Despite being an important skill, "organizational leader" is not the actual title most often given. Organizational leaders are initially termed "high potential" employees. As they move up the ranks in a company, business, or nonprofit, they then enter organizational leadership roles with managerial and director-level titles such as dean, provost, general counsel, chief financial officer, etc. The actual day-to-day tasks and responsibilities of an organizational leader include managing and motivating a team, utilizing a problem-solving mindset to address any problems that may arise, setting team goals and coordinating with other departments as broader organizational goals are being pursued.

The importance of organizational leaders is bolstering teamwork, promoting cooperation, and setting reasonable goals by making the most of the unique skill set found in their team. A possible example of organizational leadership is managing a team project researching how a company can improve its website search engine optimization (SEO). In this scenario, the leader figure will help coordinate individuals and their strengths, encourage inclusivity, and ensure a plan is set with each person taking on the responsibilities to see it through.

Some important traits for organizational leaders include:

- Problem-solving and decision making
- Clear communication and good listening
- Inclusivity and fostering a safe environment for employees
- Goal oriented
- Respect and courtesy
- Creative in utilizing the team's strengths

Leaders inspire others to act by setting good examples. Their drive and perseverance spur others on. Leaders strive to be the best they can be not to compete with others. In fact, a leader's job is to help others make their best contribution toward a shared goal. Leaders motivate others through mutual trust. The leader must trust in his or her teammates' abilities and willingness to pursue a goal. At the same time, the team must trust in their leader's ability and willingness to provide needed support. This mutual trust is essential in building a team that will be successful in reaching its goal. In today's workplace, you need to develop leadership skills to build and direct teams to get work done. Although some leadership qualities are inborn, many of the skills necessary for good leadership can be learned. In this book, we discuss ways of interacting with others that will help you lead them to success. Topics include:

- Motivating others
- Giving and taking criticism
- Organizing a project
- Delegating responsibility
- Monitoring a team's progress
- Learning leadership skills on the job

What Makes A Good Leader?

Although there are different styles of leadership, all effective leaders share certain characteristics. These are qualities that can be learned and improved upon over time.

Communication Skills

They communicate clearly. Managing a group, especially in the workplace, starts with good communication. Whether writing an e-mail or providing face-to-face employee feedback, good leaders say what they mean and mean what they say. They're not passive-aggressive, nor do they shy away from addressing challenges in a direct manner.

Passionate

They're passionate about their work. Many good leaders love what they do, and they're not afraid to show it. Of course, you can still be a good leader even if your professional and personal interests aren't a perfect match. Think about what you enjoy most in your work, and develop your enthusiasm around that you even may find that you're managing yourself into greater workplace satisfaction.

Unpopular

They don't care about being popular. In fact, if your first concern is whether everyone likes you, you may be less effective. Whether it's giving tough criticism or pointing out a practice you believe is unethical, learning how to be a good leader means getting comfortable doing or saying things that are best for your team and your organization, even if it makes you temporarily unpopular

Think Positive

They're positive and encouraging. Good leaders are uplifting. They praise employees for a job well done, taking time to coach and train if there are lapses in performance. In good times and bad, good leaders bring out the best in their employees by encouraging them to be their very best.

Connection

They build relationships. The ability to form productive connections is a key quality of a good leader. Strong managers aren't threatened by others. Instead of guarding their territory, they're constantly building bridges with others. A good leader knows the value of mutually beneficial relationships, and actively seeks them out.

Lead by Example

They lead by example. The best managers know that an essential part of what makes a good leader is setting the right example. From putting in extra hours on a major project to treating others with respect and kindness, good leaders show they're ready and willing to do anything they'd ask of their employees.

Innovation

Leaders must be able to do the job, but ability alone is not enough. True leadership requires a willingness to be bold, to consider unusual approaches to problems, to do more than just follow tried-and-true methods. Leaders are self-confident and have no need to put others down to feel good about themselves. They are willing to stand up for their ideas and debate them with others. This kind of intellectual competition is characteristic of a good leader.

Respect for Others

Balancing competition with respect may be difficult for young employees who think the way to get ahead is to outshine their coworkers. But neither workers nor supervisors like or respect leaders who think only of themselves. Above all, leadership requires the ability to get along with others in a variety of situations. For example, if you are class president, you won't be able to accomplish much if you begin to think too highly of yourself. Classmates you snub are not likely to volunteer to help with prom decorations. Likewise, if you are an assistant manager and ignore your coworkers until you need something, you will not always get the results you want.

Courteousness

Treat others as you would like to be treated. The workplace is still primarily a place where people interact. The social skills we have been practicing all our lives are important in business, too. In meetings, leaders must clearly communicate their ideas to team members, while still being open to suggestions from others. Corbis talking, avoiding sarcastic comments, and controlling emotional outbursts. Sarcasm and temper tantrums are not acceptable in a social setting and even less so in the workplace. Being in a supervisory position doesn't give you the right to be discourteous.

Sensitivity

Although they are important qualities, courtesy and agreeableness are not the only qualities of a good leader. He or she must also be sensitive to the feelings and needs of others. These needs are not always clearly expressed. Sometimes people do not even know what they want or need. Talented leaders are able to "read" the people around them and adjust their own behavior accordingly.

The aim of good management is to provide services to the community in an appropriate, efficient, equitable, and sustainable manner. This can only be achieved if key resources for service provision, including human resources, finances, hardware and process aspects of care delivery are brought together at the point of service delivery and are carefully synchronized. This chapter first discusses good management and leadership in general, then outlines relevant considerations for managing relations with patients and the district team, as well as finances and hardware and management schedules.

MANAGERS AND LEADERS

In the leadership development industry, there is a lot of confusion about the relationship between leadership and management. Many people use the terms interchangeably. Others see them as separate, but give different reasons why.

MANAGER	VS	LEADER
• gives direction		• asks questions
• has subordinates		• has followers
• holds authority		• is motivational
• tells you what		• shows you how
• has good ideas		• actions good ideas
• reacts to change		• creates change
• tries to be a hero		• makes hereos
• exercises power		• develops power

Most dictionaries suggest leadership and management are quite similar in guiding or controlling a group of people to achieve a goal. Most web articles suggest that leadership and management are different, but offer contradictory reasons, such as: leadership inspires, management plans; leaders praise, managers find fault; leaders ask questions, managers give directions; etc. However, the qualities often ascribed to leadership can also apply to managers. There can be good and bad leaders, and there can be good and bad managers.

Management and leadership are important for the delivery of good health services. Although the two are similar in some respects, they may involve different types of outlooks, skills, and behaviors. Good managers should strive to be good leaders and good leaders, need management skills to be effective.

Leaders will have a vision of what can be achieved and then communicate this to others and evolve strategies for realizing the vision. They motivate people and are able to negotiate for resources and other support to achieve their goals.

Managers ensure that the available resources are well organized and applied to produce the best results. In the resource-constrained and difficult environments of many low to middle-income countries, a manager must also be a leader to achieve optimum results.

WHAT ARE THE ATTRIBUTES OF A GOOD LEADER?

Leaders often (but not necessarily always):

- have a sense of mission;
- are charismatic;
- are able to influence people to work together for a common cause;
- are decisive;
- use creative problem solving to promote better care and a positive working environment

LEADERSHIP AND MANAGEMENT

There is an essential difference between leadership and management which is captured in these definitions:

- Leadership is setting a new direction or vision for a group that they follow, i.e.: a leader is the spearhead for that new direction.

- Management controls or directs people/resources in a group according to principles or values that have been established.

There is much more to these definitions than may at first appear. Albert Einstein said that everything should be made as simple as possible but no simpler. However, it is an oversimplification to think that leaders lead and followers follow, because the relationship between leadership, management, and followers is a complex one. Also, leadership and management are often part of the same role because there is a continual adjustment of the direction (leadership) and controlling resources to achieve that direction (management). We can see the difference more clearly by looking at some examples of leadership without management, and management without leadership.

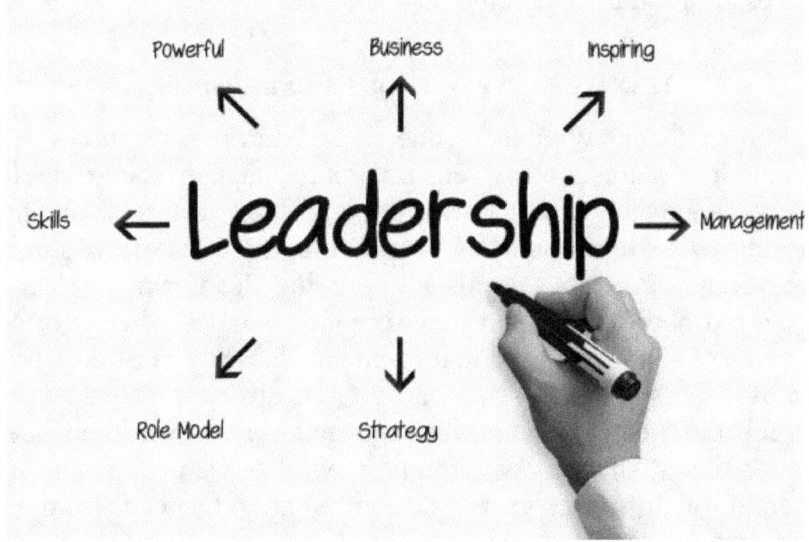

LEADERSHIP WITHOUT MANAGEMENT

The difference between leadership and management can be illustrated by considering instances when there is one without the other. Leadership without management sets a direction or vision that others follow, without considering how the new direction is going to be achieved. Other people then have to work hard in the trail that is left behind, picking up the pieces and making it work.

You can see an example of this in Lord of the Rings. At the council of Elrond, there is an argument about how they should proceed. Frodo Baggins rescues the council from the conflict by taking responsibility for destroying the ring. He sets a direction but has no idea how to go about it. During the quest, most of the management of the group comes from others, particularly Gandalf and Aragorn.

There can be leaders who don't manage in the workplace. For example, an entrepreneur might grow a business by networking, building relationships, and generating ideas for new products. However, he/she might also rely on a deputy e.g., a factory manager to ensure the right staff are recruited, products or services are produced, and the business is delivered.

MANAGEMENT WITHOUT LEADERSHIP

Management without leadership controls resources to maintain the status quo or ensure things happen according to already-established plans. For example, a sports referee manages opposing teams to ensure they keep within the rules of the game. However, a referee does not usually provide "leadership" because there is no new change, no new direction. Also, what is often referred to as "participative management" can be a very effective form of leadership. In this approach, a new direction may seem to emerge from the group rather than the leader. However, the leader has facilitated that new direction whilst also engendering ownership within the group i.e., it is an advanced form of leadership.

SYMBOLIC LEADERSHIP

Sometimes, an individual may act as a figurehead for change and be viewed as a leader even though he/she hasn't set any new direction. This can arise when a group sets a direction of its own accord, and needs a spearhead in order to express it.

In prison, Nelson Mandela was an example of symbolic leadership. Although his ability to take action was limited, he continued to grow in power and influence (as the symbolic leader for the anti-apartheid movement). This power came from the mass movement, from the group that are nominally viewed as the followers. Following his release from prison, he demonstrated actual leadership by leading South Africa into a process of reconciliation rather than retribution. This illustrates the complexity of the relationship between leaders, followers, and context. A leader's power often comes from the followers. For example, in democratic government, leaders are elected because of the direction they offer e.g., for economic growth or social development. However, if they subsequently pursue a direction that is different from the expectations of the electorate, they may lose the next election, or even provoke civil unrest beforehand.

LEADERSHIP STYLES

There are many different types of leadership (or management) style. Different situations, groups, or cultures, may require the use of different styles in order to set a direction or ensure that it is followed.

BEING INNOVATIVE

As leadership involves setting a new visionary direction e.g., JFK setting the goal of putting a man on the moon. As management involves producing creative ideas to ensure the vision is realized e.g., coming up with ideas that enabled Apollo 13 to return safely to earth.

PARTICIPATIVE MANAGEMENT

As leadership involves facilitating a new direction through team discussion. As management involves winning the commitment of a team to a defined goal. Everyone has their own preferred set of leadership styles. One aspect of becoming an effective is to build greater awareness of those styles, learning how to harness them productively, and mitigating natural weaknesses.

ORGANIZATIONAL GOVERNANCE

The key ingredients to project management are people, processes, and technology. Technology is a tool, while processes provide a structure and path for managing and carrying out the project. The success of a project, however, is often determined by the various project stakeholders, as well as who is (or who is not) on the project team. In this chapter, we will discuss the human resources of project management. The area of project human resource management entails:

- organizational planning
- staff acquisition
- team development.

Project Organization

Key project management committees that are responsible for project delivery and implementation

ORGANIZATION PLANNING

Organization planning focuses on the roles, responsibilities, and relationships among the project stakeholders. These individuals or groups can be internal or external to the project. Moreover, organizational planning involves creating a project structure that will support the project processes and stakeholders so that the project is carried out efficiently and effectively.

STAFF ACQUISITION

Staff acquisition includes staffing the project with the best available human resources. Effective staffing involves having policies, procedures, and practices to guide the recruitment of appropriately skilled and experienced staff. Moreover, it may include negotiating for staff from other functional areas within the organization.

TEAM DEVELOPMENT

Team development involves creating an environment to develop and support the individual team members and the team itself.

This chapter will expand upon these three subjects and integrate several relatively recent concepts for understanding the governance structure in project management. Three primary organizational structure: the functional, project, and matrix will be described. In addition, the various opportunities and challenges for projects conducted under each structure will be discussed. As an Engineering Manager or project team member, it is important to understand an organization's structure since this will determine authorities, roles, responsibilities, communication channels, and availability of resources.

Nothing can be achieved without team effort

In Project Management, the project team carries out the work needed to complete the project.

Once the project team is in place, it is important that the project team learn from each other and from past project experiences. Thus, the idea of learning cycles will be introduced as a tool for team learning and for capturing lessons learned that can be documented, stored, and retrieved using a knowledge management system

PROJECT STAKEHOLDERS

Stakeholders are individuals, groups, or even organizations that have a stake, or claim, in the project's outcome. Often, we think of stakeholders as only those individuals or groups having an interest in the successful outcome of a project, but the sad truth is that there are many who can gain from a project's failure. While the formal organization tells us a little about the stakeholders and what their interests may be, the informal organization paints a much more interesting picture.

Budget Management

Engineering Manager must be capable to prepare the project budget. All businesses have a responsibility to the monies they are allotted, have earned, and have acquired through donations. In project management, the work completed within a project must be measured for value and accounted for. The budget the organization has set for the project must be guarded. Ultimately, the success of the project should generate an increase in funds, productivity, or efficiency for the sponsoring organization.

Project Resources

Engineering Manager must be organized. How much time has been wasted looking for documentation, contracts, or permits? How much money has been lost due to disorganization? How many projects have failed because the Engineering Manager did not keep and maintain accurate records? Organization is a methodical approach to storing and retrieving information, as it is needed. Organization does not require a spotless desk, thousands of labeled file folders, or archives of every project-related document. Organization requires thorough, fast, and reliable access to project data.

Team Leadership

Managing a project team is different than leading a project team. It has been said that you manage things, but lead people. In project management, you must create a relationship between the project team members and yourself to excite, motivate, and inspire the workers to move toward the strategy and vision of the project deliverable.

PEOPLE MANAGEMENT

People management requires several soft skills, including those that can lead to open and honest communication as well as improved employee experience. Each of these skills can better help you interact with your employees and perform organizational tasks.

Here are eight essential people management skills to incorporate into your workplace:

- Empowering employees
- Active listening
- Conflict-resolution
- Flexibility
- Patience
- Clear communication
- Trust
- Organization

EMPOWERING EMPLOYEES

Empowering your employees helps them develop new skills and be more productive. It's important to train new employees well and give them the knowledge and resources they need to perform assigned tasks and continue learning on their own.

Other important aspects of empowering employees include:

- Offering constructive feedback to encourage skill-building
- Being available for questions or additional training
- Allowing them to adjust workflow or standard processes if it improves their productivity

- Encouraging them to take additional skill-building courses and learning opportunities
- Supporting them on or managing challenging projects

ACTIVE LISTENING

Active listening is the practice of listening to the speaker to fully understand their perspective, question or concern before responding. Active listeners remove distractions, maintain eye contact and offer verbal or non-verbal cues to indicate their engagement and understanding. When an employee comes to you with a question or issue, use nonverbal cues such as nodding to demonstrate your engagement while they're speaking. Respond thoughtfully by repeating a summary of your understanding of their message.

If you have understood, you can then ask follow-up questions to learn more about what they need. You can also express that you empathize with their experience to further assure them you understand and respect them. These active listening techniques lead to quality people management that promotes positive interactions in the workplace.

CONFLICT-RESOLUTION

Good conflict-resolution skills can help address interpersonal challenges. You can analyze the situation and identify what the causes of the conflict might be. If there's a miscommunication or differing opinions, you can mediate between opposing parties and help them make a compromise or reach a collective understanding. After mediation, monitor the situation to ensure the conflict is fully resolved and to prevent it from occurring again.

Flexibility

Knowing when to be flexible and when to more firmly direct employees is an important aspect of effective people management. You can demonstrate flexibility in your management style by accommodating individual employee needs such as adjustable schedules or remote work options—and allowing employees to adjust their individual workflow so they can be as productive as possible. You should assess the results of the employee's process to ensure its efficiency and to help them revise the process if it can be optimized. For example, if one of your employees prefers to complete related tasks in batches while another employee moves back and forth between different tasks, analyze each employee's results. If both employees are their most productive using their respective processes, then you can encourage them to continue using and improving their systems. You may even ask them to demonstrate their individual processes to other employees to optimize the entire team's workflow. If an employee seems to be struggling with personalizing their process, you can coach them through the standard steps, and help them discover what works best for them.

Patience

Patience is an important people management skill that uses kindness, respect and empathy while helping others overcome obstacles. You can use patience when training new employees, teaching new processes, handling conflicts or solving problems. When employees can trust their managers to be patient, they are more likely to ask for clarification to ensure they understand directions and to increase the quality of their work. For example, if an employee continues asking questions about a single process, you should continue to guide them while trying new ways to better communicate your message. Consider providing multiple examples that clarify and demonstrate your instructions, or combine typed instructions with visual diagrams if possible.

Clear Communication

Communication is a necessary people management skill that enables team members to work together in solving problems, brainstorming new ideas and adapting to new changes. Your ability to clearly communicate with your coworkers can help you be a better team member. Practice effective communication by using clear and simple language so every recipient understands your message. Consider revising the way you give your message to avoid common barriers, such as too much information at one time or inaccessible terms. Allow your employees to ask clarifying questions, and directly confirm that each member of your team understands the information so there is no miscommunication.

Trust

Trust means believing that you can rely on someone's abilities, assistance or advice when you need it most. Building trust helps your team work together more efficiently and productively. Teams should be able to trust that their leader supports them and believes in their hard work. Leaders should be able to trust that their team can complete tasks correctly and on time. You can build trust by reliably performing your tasks and demonstrating technical skills when employees ask for help. You can also promote trust when you provide constructive feedback that helps team members improve their skills and work quality.

ORGANIZATION

Managing a team involves handling several different ongoing tasks simultaneously. Being organized is an important people management skill that helps you track and maintain your team's productivity. Signs of effective organization include:

- Promptly responding to emails, approval requests and questions
- Keeping a calendar to actively track deadlines
- Running meetings that efficiently discuss information
- Properly assigning tasks to team members
- See your instant resume report on Indeed
- Get recommendations for your resume in minutes

How To Develop Your People Management Skills

If you can demonstrate your people management skills, you can become a stronger candidate for future leadership roles. Identifying your strengths and areas for improvement can help you decide which distinct skills to grow. Consider using these strategies to develop specific people management skills:

Choose individual skills to focus on: People management is a broad skill set. Select a specific skill from the list above, such as conflict resolution, and learn more about the skill, its benefits and how to apply it in the workplace. Enroll in professional development courses: Some companies offer their own management training programs while others may sponsor employees to take professional development courses elsewhere. You can find courses online or through an educational institution. Find a mentor or business coach: Specialized or targeted attention is a great way to develop people management skills quickly. Mentors and business coaches can give you personalized feedback and specific, actionable strategies. Ask other managers for feedback or advice: Ask your manager or supervisor for advice on how to develop your people management skills and potential leadership opportunities where you can demonstrate and practice those skills.

What Is Team Management?

Team management is a manager or organization's ability to lead a group of people in accomplishing a task or common goal. Effective team management involves supporting, communicating with and uplifting team members so they perform to the best of their abilities and continue to grow as professionals. Precisely what constitutes effective team management, however, may differ depending on the work environment and the people. Some managers do well with an authoritative approach, while other managers prefer to manage their teams in a more casual way. Some team members may also respond differently to certain management styles. Understanding your own leadership style and what works best with your team is an important part of team management.

Why Is Team Management Important?

Team management is important for a number of reasons within the workplace:

- It promotes a unified approach to leadership within a company or team, especially when team building is implemented.
- It makes it easier to solve problems through the implementation of negotiating and critical thinking.
- It encourages open communication between managers and team members and emphasizes good communication skills and active listening.

- It ensures managers and team members are working toward a common goal that has been clearly defined.

It helps managers clearly outline the roles and expectations for their team members. Understanding the importance of team management and working to develop your team management skills can help you be the most effective leader possible. The more effective you're at managing your team, the more successful your team will be within the workplace.

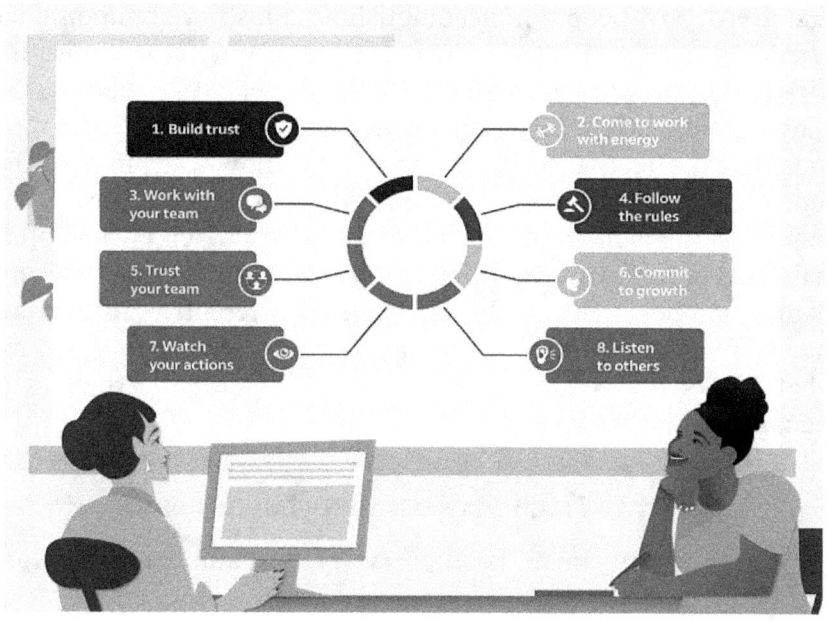

EXAMPLES OF EFFECTIVE TEAM MANAGEMENT SKILLS

Effective team managers tend to share certain skills, attitudes and tactics. Although good management involves more than merely applying a list of tried-and-tested methods and approaches, you may benefit from considering practices that have worked well for other managers over the years. If you're new in management or wish to grow your management skills, here are a few ways you can hone your skills as a team leader as well as real-life examples within the workplace.

FOCUS ON SERVING RATHER THAN MANAGING

Although it may seem counter-intuitive, effective managers focus on serving rather than managing their teams. As a manager, you should at all times have the best interests of your team members in mind and should strive to assist and support them in achieving both individual and team goals. In addition, a good manager leads through actions, as opposed to merely giving orders and delegating tasks. If you want your team to act professionally and deliver excellent work, you should act accordingly and set an example.

Example: A team member has phoned to say she is ill and not coming into work. Instead of adding all of her outstanding tasks to the workload of other team members, you offer to complete some of the tasks yourself.

DON'T ALWAYS ASSUME YOU'RE RIGHT

If you want to be a good manager, you have to be open to continuously learning. While as a manager you may occupy a more senior position than the team members you manage, you should keep an open mind as to what your employees can teach you on a daily basis. Apart from learning from your team, you should also ensure that you stay up-to-date with the latest trends and developments and invest in your own ongoing professional development.

Example: During a meeting with your team, you give your opinion about a technical issue that one of your clients is experiencing. One of your senior technicians responds to your analysis with a different point of view. Instead of immediately assuming your viewpoint is correct, you listen attentively to what he has to say and then have a constructive discussion on the matter.

Make Transparency A Priority

A transparent workplace can help employees feel more connected and encourage creativity and accountability. Practicing transparency through open and consistent communication allows your team members to feel a sense of respect which is important for overall job satisfaction and productivity. This can also help your team members have more confidence when it comes to contributing ideas and solutions to the workplace, which can ultimately benefit everyone involved.

Example: Rather than distributing team tasks on an individual basis, use a project management system to assign and display tasks and overall goals for a particular project. When team members can clearly see their roles in a project and know exactly what their responsibilities are, they are more likely to hold themselves accountable for producing quality work.

Set Boundaries

Although you want to treat your team with kindness and respect, it is also important to set boundaries and assert your authority at times. Team members should know that your job is to ensure their work gets done efficiently and that, when necessary, you will take disciplinary action. There should be a very clear understanding of responsibilities and roles within the workspace to discourage team members from challenging unclear boundaries.

Example: A client has informed you that one of your technicians has not been attending to the necessary maintenance tasks on a regular basis as per their service agreement. Rather than sending an email to let your technician know they need to update the maintenance tasks, you meet with them in person to clearly outline your expectations and discuss the employee's recent unsatisfactory performance. By meeting in person, you show your team member that you take their performance seriously and that not following through on work assignments will not be tolerated.

PROVIDE A POSITIVE WORKSPACE

Although the business world is a serious place that often involves profit margins, risk assessments and performance evaluations, studies have shown that a bit of humor and light-heartedness in the office can have a remarkably positive effect on productivity. If possible, organize fun work outings or liven up the office environment with some plants and bright colors. Even if you just bring a bunch of flowers to work or tell a joke every now and then, this can brighten your team's day and foster a culture of happiness within the workspace.

Example: The morale in the office is a bit low after losing a big account. You decide to lighten up the mood by hiring a mobile massage therapist to give everyone a shoulder and neck massage. When everyone is a bit more relaxed you sit them down with doughnuts and coffee to discuss lessons learned and how the team can improve on service delivery in the future.

EMPHASIZE CONSTANT AND EFFECTIVE COMMUNICATION WITHIN THE WORKPLACE

One of the most important aspects of effective management is communication. As a manager, you should provide your team with all the relevant information at all times as well as encourage feedback from your employees. As effective communication starts with attentive listening, you should set an example to your team members by really listening to them and considering their opinions and input. You should also strive to foster a work environment where team members have the freedom to express themselves in a polite and respectful manner. Constructive and positive communication does, however, not always involve talking in person. There is an array of social media apps available today through which co-workers can stay in touch with each other and exchange ideas.

Example: You realize there is a lack of communication in the office, which is negatively affecting service delivery. To address this issue, you call a meeting with team members where you discuss processes and where the breakdown in communication is taking place. To assist team members, you provide them with a mobile application on their phones where they can input the necessary updates when they are working outside of the office space.

ENCOURAGE AND NURTURE YOUR TEAM'S GROWTH

As a manager, you should support and nurture your team. Your staff should know you have their personal development and best interests at heart and that you're supportive of their goals and dreams. This means that you should always be on the lookout for ways to develop and enrich your team, such as providing them with opportunities to attend workshops and conferences and stay up-to-date through training and certification. Apart from encouraging your workers to continuously expand their knowledge, you can also nurture and motivate them through positive feedback for good work or improvement in performance. However, you should also provide constructive criticism at times, as this can assist team members in their professional development.

Example: An exciting conference is taking place which involves new technology. Although only senior engineers and management typically attend conferences, you have a talented junior engineer in your team who can benefit from going to the conference. You decide to raise this matter in the next management meeting and request that they allow the junior engineer to attend.

BE OPEN TO CHANGE

To be an effective manager you need to be open to change. This involves adapting your management style when necessary and realizing that different team members may have different approaches and ways of doing things. Be open to trying new technologies and to changing your typical method of management when it no longer produces the desired outcomes.

POSITIVE WAYS TO LEAD BY EXAMPLE IN THE WORKPLACE

A workplace can benefit from having influential leaders in place to guide employees. As a leader, your team looks to you for inspiration, encouragement and direction. You can provide this by leading by example and building a culture of trust and accountability. Leading by example means guiding others through your behaviors and inspiring them to do the same as you. It is a leadership style servant leadership where you model the behavior you want to see in your team.

When you lead by example, you provide a path to direct others so that everyone works toward a goal with the same purpose. A leader makes it natural for people to feel like they want to do the best for the organization they work for. Leading by example can accomplish this and create a workplace filled with trust, confidence and purpose.

BENEFITS OF LEADING BY EXAMPLE IN THE WORKPLACE

Many benefits come from leading by example whether you're an executive or a junior associate. The benefits of having someone or multiple people in the workplace who led by example include:

MORE RESPECT AND TRUST

Someone who leads by example can expect to receive respect from their superiors, people who work alongside them and their employees. They are able to:

- Inspire confidence in others
- Understand the workplace and how everyone works together
- Stick to their word and actively seek solutions to problems
- Form a workplace culture that celebrates everyone's skill set
- Involve every member of the team in projects or important decisions

HIGHER PRODUCTIVITY

When you lead by example, your team will soon follow, working just as hard and accomplishing just as much as you to do their part for the organization. They will strive to make their team proud and not let anyone down by performing below their abilities.

LOYAL EMPLOYEES

Leading by example inspires those around you to enjoy being part of the team and a company employee. They want to enjoy the people they work with, including their leader. Satisfied employees have lower absenteeism, are more positive, contribute more to discussions, volunteer to take on more projects or help a coworker.

COMMITMENT TO THE ORGANIZATION

When there is positive leadership, employees are generally more committed to the company. They strive to help achieve its goals, develop a team mentality and work to support the company's mission, purpose and values. When a leader leads by example and works alongside their team, they inspire others to do the same.

BENCHMARK STANDARDS

A leader's actions set the standard for behavior in the workplace. How you act can determine how team members respond. For example, if you're always on time for meetings, your team will be more likely to do the same. On the other hand, if you don't communicate with your employees, you may notice the workplace becomes siloed and non-collaborative.

Chapter 5 : PROJECT MANAGEMENT

Moving toward a role as an Engineering Manager requires skills in project management. A project involves a group of inter-related activities that are planned and then executed in a certain sequence to create a unique product or service within a specific timeframe, to achieve benefits. Projects are often critical components of an organization's business strategy. Projects vary in size and complexity.

For example, they may:

- Involve changes to existing systems, policies, legislation and/or procedures
- Entail organizational change
- Involve a single person or many people
- Involve a single unit of one organization, or may span cross organizational boundaries
- Involve engagement and management of external resources
- Require less than 100 hours or take several years

PROJECTS VERSUS OPERATIONS

In some organizations, everything is a project. In other organizations, projects are rare exercises in change. There's a fine line between projects and operations, and often these entities overlap in function. Consider the following points shared by projects and operations:

- Both involve employees
- Both typically have limited resources: people, money, or both
- Both are hopefully designed, executed, and managed by someone in charge

So, what is a project and how do you know if you are managing one? A project as 'a temporary endeavor was undertaken to create a unique product or service.' Temporary means that the project has an end date. Unique means that the project's end result is different than the results of other functions of the organization. Often projects are confused with general business duties: marketing, sales, manufacturing, and so on. The tell-tale sign of a project is that is has an end date and that it's unique from other activities within the organization.

Some examples of projects include:

- Designing a new product or service
- Converting from one computer application to another
- Building a new warehouse
- Moving from one building to another
- Organizing a political campaign
- Designing and building a new airplane

The output of projects can result in operations. For example, imagine a company creating a new airplane. This new airplane will be a small personal plane that would allow people to fly to different destinations with the same freedom they use in driving their car. The project team will have to design an airplane from scratch that may be similar to a car. This project, to create a personal plane, is temporary, but not necessarily short term. It may take years to go from concept to completion but the project does have an end date. A project of this magnitude may require hundreds of prototypes before a working model are ready for the marketplace. In addition, there are countless regulations, safety issues, and quality control issues that must be pacified before completion.

Once the initial plane is designed, built, and approved, the end result of the project is business operations. As the company creates a new vehicle, it would follow through with their design by manufacturing, marketing, selling, supporting, and improving their product. The initial design of the airplane is the project-the business of manufacturing it, supporting sold units, and marketing the product constitutes the ongoing operations part of business.

Operations are the day-to-day work that goes on in the organization. A manufacturer manufactures things, scientists' complete research and development, and businesses provide goods and services. Operations are the heart of organizations. Projects, on the other hand, are short-term endeavor that fall outside of the normal day-to-day operations an organization offers.

Once the project is completed, the project team moves along to other projects and activities. The people who are actually building the aero planes on the assembly line however have no end date in sight, and will continue to create aero planes as longs as there is a demand for the product.

PROJECT MANAGEMENT BODY OF KNOWLEDGE

Project management is the supervision and control of the work required to complete the project vision. The project team carries out the work needed to complete the project, while the project manager schedules, monitors, and controls the various project tasks. Projects, being the temporary and unique things that they are, require the project manager to be actively involved with the project implementation. They are not self-propelled. Project management is comprised of the following ten knowledge management areas:

- **Integration Management** include includes unification, consolidation, communication, and the integrative actions to control project execution, to manage stakeholder expectations, and to meet project requirements.
- **Scope Management** include the process of creating the project scope document that describe the scope of the project and the

scope of the product. The key benefit of this process is that it provides guidance and direction on how scope will be managed throughout the project.

- **Time Management** deals with the ability to plan and finish the project in a timely manner. It involved defining project activities, estimating the resources required to perform the work, estimating the duration of activities, scheduling activities and ensuring adherence to the project schedule.

- **Cost Management** include the processes that establish the policies, procedures, and documentation for planning, managing, expending, and controlling project costs. The key benefit of this process is that it provides guidance and direction on how the project costs will be managed throughout the project.

- **Quality Management** is to ensure that the project outputs are delivered fit-for-purpose. If outputs are not fit-for-purpose there is a possibility that planned project benefits will not be realized, or realized to a much lesser extent. It can be achieved by developing quality criteria for the outputs themselves and by ensuring that all project management processes are conducted in a quality manner.

- **Human Resource Management** involve planning for managing the people, finances, and physical and information resources required to perform the project activities is vital, no matter what the project size or complexity. For small projects, this planning may not be documented, but for large and/or more complex projects, detailed documentation will enable better management of the resources, as well as transparency for the key stakeholders.

Project management processes in the absence of appropriate project management knowledge areas will not be sufficient to take a project through the respective phases of the project life cycle. The Project Management Competency comprised of 10 knowledge areas that integrate with 47 project management processes.

- **Communications Management** includes the processes involved in developing an appropriate approach and plan for project communications based on stakeholder's information needs and requirements, and available organizational assets.
- **Stakeholder Management** involve the identification of people or organizations that have an interest in the project processes, outputs, outcomes or benefits, and planning for how their involvement will be managed on an ongoing basis. It may be done very quickly for a small project, whereas a large and/or more complex project will require a formal stakeholder analysis, a Stakeholder Management Plan as part of the Project Business Plan and ongoing monitoring and review of progress. Stakeholder Management is closely related to communication strategy and planning.
- **Risk Management** describe the processes concerned with identifying, analyzing and responding to project risk. It consists of risk identification, risk analysis, risk evaluation and risk treatment. The processes are iterative throughout the life of the project and should be built into the project management

planning and activities. For small projects, a brief scan and ongoing monitoring may be all that is required. For large and/or more complex projects, a formalized system for analyzing, managing and reporting should be established, including the use of a Risk Register.

- **Procurement Management** include the processes associated with contract management and change control processes required to develop and administer contracts or purchase orders issued by authorized project team members; administer any contract issued by an outside organization (the buyer) that is acquiring deliverables from the project.

PROJECT MANAGEMENT LIFE CYCLE AND PROCESSES

One common attribute of all projects is that they eventually end. Think back to one of your favorite projects. The project started with a desire to change something within an organization. The idea to change this 'something' was mulled around, kicked around, and researched until someone with power deemed it a good idea to move forward and implement the project. As the project progressed towards completion there were some very visible phases within the project life. Each phase within the life of the project created a deliverable. For example, consider a project to build a new warehouse. The construction company has some pretty clear phases within this project: research, blueprints, approvals and permits, breaking ground, laying the foundation, and so on. Each phase, big or small, results in some accomplishment that everyone can look to and say, 'Hey! We're making progress!' Eventually the project is completed and the warehouse is put into production. At the beginning of the project, through planning, research, experience, and expert judgment, the project manager and the project team will plot out when each phase should begin, when it should end, and the related deliverable that will come from each phase. Often, the deliverable of each phase is called a milestone. The milestone is a significant point in the schedule that allows the stakeholders to see how far the project has progressed-and how far the project has to go to reach completion.

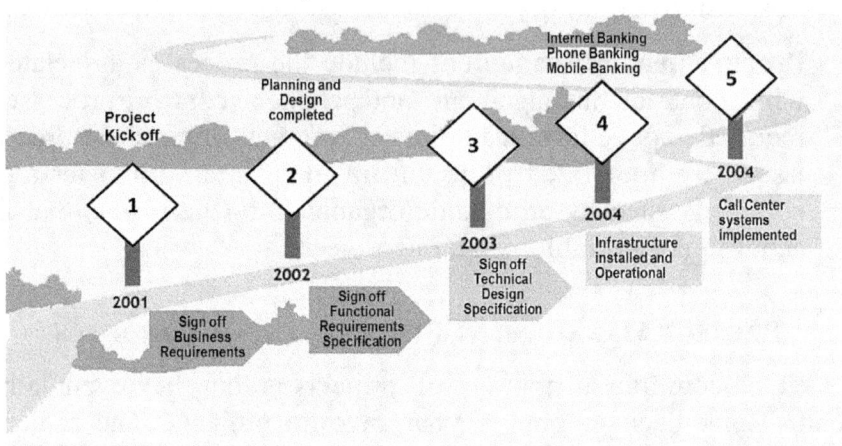

EXAMINING THE PROJECT LIFE CYCLE

By now, you're more than familiar with the concept of a project's life cycle. You also know each project is different and that there are some attributes common across all project life cycles. For example, the concept of breaking the project apart into manageable phases to move towards completion is typical across most projects. As we've discussed, at the completion of a project phase, an inspection or audit is usually completed. This inspection confirms the project is in alignment with the requirements and expectations of the customer. If the results of the audit or briefing are not in alignment, then rework can happen, new expectations may be formulated, or the project may be killed.

WORKING THROUGH THE PROJECT LIFE CYCLE

Project life cycles, comprised of phases, move the project along. Project life cycles allow a project manager to determine several things about the project, such as:

- What work will be completed in each phase of the project?
- What resources, people, equipment, and facilities will be needed within each phase?
- What are the expected deliverables of each phase?
- What is the expected cost to complete a project phase?
- Which phases contain the highest amount of risk?

Armed with the appropriate information for each project phase, the project manager can plan for cost, schedules, resource availability, risk management, and other project management activities to ensure that the project progresses successfully.

CHARACTERISTICS OF A PROJECT

Characteristics of a "Project"

A project is a temporary endeavor undertaken to create a unique Product or Service. Temporary means that every project has a definite beginning and a definite end.

- Have clear requirements
- Have an agreed scope of work
- Have a defined schedule
- Have an approved budget
- Involve resources
- Have some degree of risk
- Produce outcome / benefit
- Create a product or service
- Unique
- Have assumptions and constraints

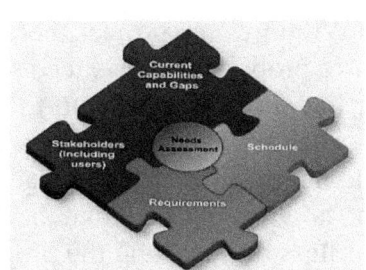

Most projects have similar characteristics, such as the following:

They Are Demanding

The stakeholders, the people with a vested interested in the project, are all going to have different expectations, needs, and requests of the project deliverables. No doubt there will be conflict between the stakeholders.

They Have Clear Requirements

Projects should have a clearly defined set of requirements. These requirements will set the bar for the actual product or service created by the project, the quality of the project, and the timeliness of the project's completion.

They Come with Assumptions

Projects also have assumptions. Assumptions are beliefs held to be true, but that haven't been proven. For example, the project may be operating under the assumption that the project team will have access to do the work at any time during the workday, rather than only in the evenings or weekends.

Constraints are Imposed

Within every project there is a driving force for the project. You've probably experienced some force first-hand. For example, ever had a project that had to be done by an exact date or you'd face fines and fees? This is a schedule constraint. Or a project that could not go over its set budget? This is a financial constraint. Or what about a project that had to hit an exact level of quality regardless of how long the project took? This is scope constraint. All are forces that tend to be in competition with each other.

PROJECT CONSTRAINTS

Project constraints influence practically all areas of the project process. Consider constraints as a ruling requirement over the project. Common constraints you'll encounter are time constraints in the form of deadlines and the availability of resources.

Specifically, there are four major constraints that a project manager will encounter:

SCOPE

The scope of the project constitutes the parameters of what the project will, and will not, include. As the project progresses, the stakeholders may try to change the project scope to include more requirements than what was originally planned for (commonly called scope creep). Of course, if you change the project scope to include more deliverables, the project will likely need more time and/or money to be completed.

SCHEDULE

This is the expected time when the project will be completed. Realistic schedules don't come easily. As you may have experienced, some projects require a definite end date rather than, or in addition to, a definite budget. For example, imagine a manufacturer creating a new product for a tradeshow. The tradeshow is not going to change the start date of the show just because the manufacturer is running late with their production schedule.

COST

Budgets, monies, greenbacks, whatever you want to call it-the cost of completing the project is always high on everyone's list of questions. The project manager must find a method to accurately predict the cost of completing the project within a given timeline, and then control the project to stay within the given budget.

QUALITY

What good is a project if it is finished on time and on budget, but the quality of the deliverable is so poor it is unusable? Some projects have a set level of quality that allows the project team to aim for. Other projects follow the organization's Quality Assurance Program such as ISO 9000. And, unfortunately, some projects have a general, vague idea of what an acceptable level of quality is. Without a specific target for quality, trouble can ensue. The project manager and project team may spend more time and monies to hit an extremely high level of quality when a lower, expected level of quality would suffice for the project.

> **Constraints are limits or boundaries that is affecting your project activity. Constraints will affect the project scheduling activity.**

Category	Example of Constraints
Resources	• Computer resources will be available on a limited basis.
	• Test environment will not be available on Mondays.
Delivery	• All project documents will require 10 working days for review.
	• Hardware delivery lead times cannot be confirmed.
Budget	• Local travelling expenses is limited to $500 per month per individual.
	• Project entertainment expenses is subject to Sponsor's approval

Chapter 6 : PROJECT MANAGEMENT PROCESSES

On a project, project, there are fundamental activities that must happen before the work begins. The rules, management principles, planning, and general guidelines for a project are the project management framework. The project management framework is the skeleton of projects. And, just like a house, even though every project has a general framing, the end results are typically different. The management of a project, the day-to-day activities, is the bones of successful project management. A project manager must monitor, maintain, and control the work of the project to ensure timeliness, accountability, quality, and success. Just as you wouldn't randomly build a home without plans and a level of control, a project requires a level of detail and management to guarantee completion and acceptability.

The five processes of a project are initiation, planning, execution, control, and closure. The five processes interact with one another and allow the project manager, the project sponsor, the project team, and even the stakeholders to witness the progress, success, and, sometimes, failure of a project. These processes are cyclic, iterative, progressively elaborated, documentation, and project manager participation.

WHAT IS PROJECT MANAGEMENT PROCESS?

A process is a set of interrelated actions and activities performed to create a specific product, service, or result. Each process is characterized by its inputs, the tools and techniques that can be applied, and the resulting outputs. Each process has several Tasks or Activities. Resources will be assigned to each Task.

- Initiating processes are processes used to initiate a project or phase once commitment is obtained.

- Planning processes are processes used to develop and maintain a workable plan to support the project's overall goal.

- Executing processes are processes used to coordinate people and other resources to execute the work described in the project plan.
- Controlling processes are processes used to ensure proper control and reporting mechanisms are in place so that progress can be monitored, problems identified, and appropriate actions taken when necessary.
- Closing processes are processes used to provide closure in terms of a formal acceptance that the project or a project's phase has been completed satisfactorily.

PROCESSES ASSOCIATED WITH INITIATION PHASE

- Initiating the Project
- Define Scope
- Define Schedule
- Define Quality
- Define Cost
- Perform Risk Identification
- Develop Initial Project Plan
- Review Initiation phase

PROCESSES ASSOCIATED WITH PLANNING PHASE

- Initiating Planning phase
- Verify Scope
- Verify Schedule
- Plan Quality Assurance
- Refine Budget
- Perform Risk Assessment
- Refine Project Plan
- Review Planning phase

PROCESSES ASSOCIATED WITH EXECUTION PHASE

- Manage Change Control
- Manage Acceptance
- Manage Risks
- Manage Issues
- Manage Communications
- Manage Organizational Change
- Manage Project Team
- Manage Project Transition

PROCESSES ASSOCIATED WITH CONTROLLING PHASE

- Control Scope
- Control Schedule
- Control Quality
- Control Costs
- Control Risks
- Control Communications
- Acquire Acceptance

PROCESSES ASSOCIATED WITH THE CLOSING PHASE

- Conduct Post-Implementation Review
- Perform Administrative Closeout

INPUT-PROCESS-OUTPUT MODEL

It is imperative initially to define a project in terms of the outputs and benefits the project should achieve. It helps to link directly the actual outputs of the project and project activities with the organizational goals and directions of an organization.

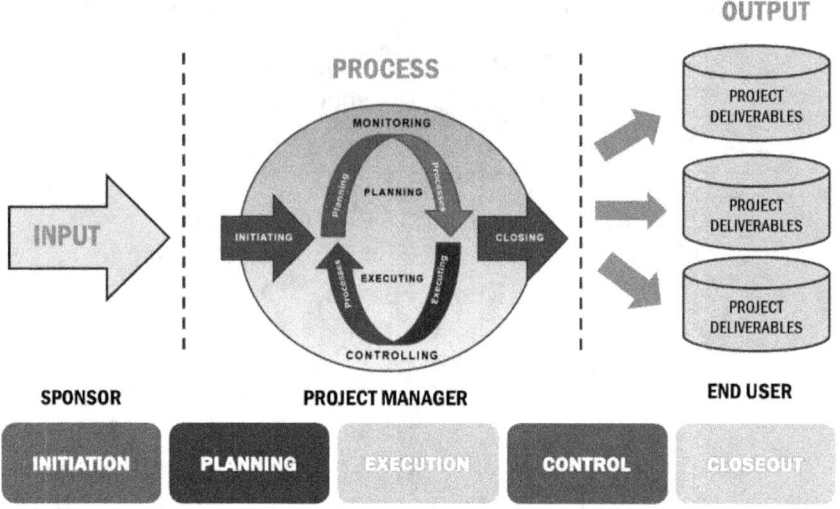

A project uses inputs example resources, budgets, material, it can also be document resulted from a previous process. The Project Manager normally manages the process to deliver agreed project outputs in the form of services or products. Customers, through utilization, transform the project outputs into the desired project benefits.

The following Input-Process-Output Model diagram illustrates the way the work or components in a project are undertaken - from left to right.

In the example below, the Project Scope Statement derived from Project Initiation phase will be an input into the process "Verify Scope" to produce the output called "Project Scope".

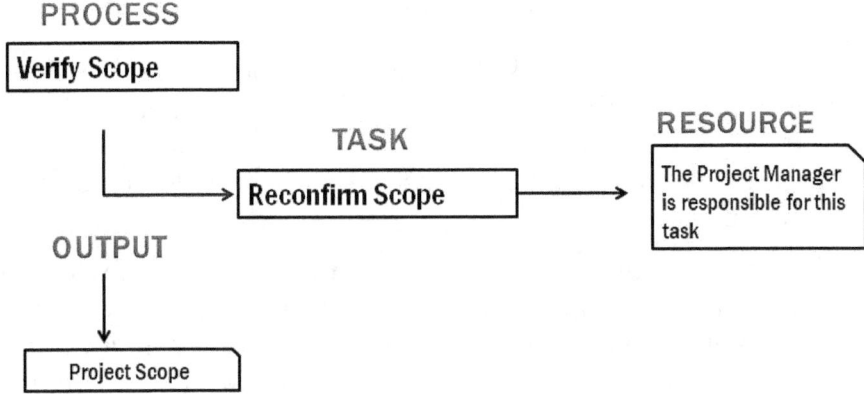

Outputs are the new or revised products or services delivered by the project to the Business Owners. They are usually expressed at a high-level and can be broken down into various components or deliverables.

In determining the project outputs, fitness-for-purpose or quality criteria should also be determined.

Chapter 7 : PROJECT LIFE CYCLE AND PHASES

The project life cycle (PLC) is a collection of logical stages or phases that maps the life of a project from its beginning to its end in order to define, build, and deliver the product of a project that is the information system. Each phase should provide one or more deliverables.

A **deliverable** is a tangible and verifiable product of work (ex. project plan, design specifications, delivered system, et cetera.). Deliverables at the end of each phase also provide tangible benefits throughout the project and serve to define the work and resources needed for each phase.

Projects should be broken up into phases to make the project more manageable and to reduce risk. Stage gates are the phase-end review of key deliverables that allow the organization to evaluate the project's performance and to take immediate action to correct any errors or problems. Although the deliverables at the end of a stage or phase usually are approved before proceeding to the next stage, fast-tracking or starting the next phase before approval is obtained can sometimes reduce the project's schedule. Overlapping phases can be risky and should only be done when the risk is deemed acceptable.

In a typical project management life cycle, there are five phases:

- Initiation
- Planning
- Executing
- Controlling
- Closing

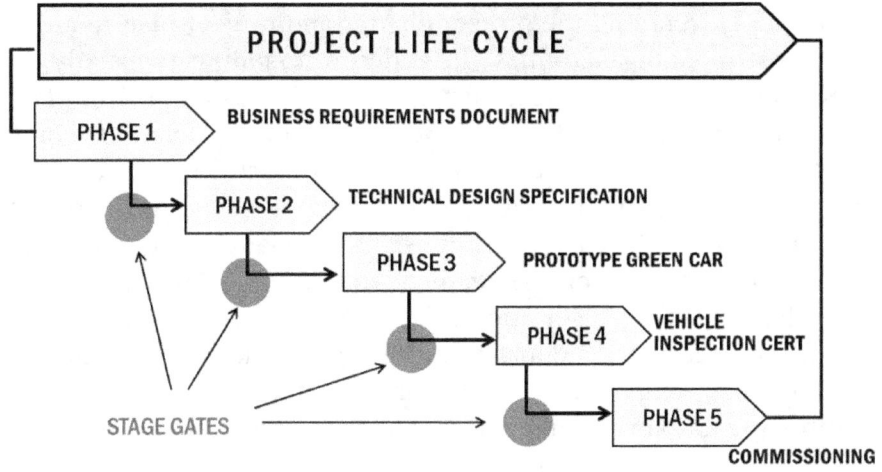

INITIATION PHASE

The phase signals the beginning of the project. It requires an organization to make a commitment in terms of time and resources. For example, the first phase of the project methodology recommends the development of a business case to identify several viable alternatives that can support a particular organization's strategy and goals. In short, the time and effort needed to develop the business case does not come without a cost. One can measure this cost directly in terms of the labor cost and time spent, and indirectly by the time and effort that could have been devoted to some other endeavor.

PLANNING PHASE

Planning is the most crucial part of any project. Since projects are undertaken to create something of value that generally has not been done before, the planning process is of critical importance. The planning process should be in line with the size and complexity of the project, that is, larger, complex projects may require a greater planning effort than smaller, less complex projects. Developing the project charter and project plan requires the most planning activities. In addition, planning is usually an iterative process. A project manager may develop a project plan, but senior management or the client may not approve the scope, budget, or schedule. In addition, planning is still more of an art than a science. Experience and good judgment are just as important as, and perhaps even more important to quality planning than, using the latest project management software tool. It is important that the project manager and project team develop a realistic and useful project plan. Supporting processes include scope planning, activity planning, resource planning, cost estimating, schedule estimating, organizational planning, and procurement planning.

EXECUTING PHASE

Once the project plan has been developed and approved, it is time to execute the activities of the project plan. The product-oriented processes play an important role when completing the project plan activities. For example, the tools and methods for developing and/or implementing a system become critical for achieving the project's end result. Supporting processes include quality assurance, risk management, team development, and an implementation plan. Although executing processes are part of every project phase, the majority of the executing processes will occur during the execution and control phase of the project methodology.

CONTROLLING PHASE

The controlling processes allow for managing and measuring the progress towards the project's measurable organizational value (MOV) and the scope, schedule, budget, and quality objectives. Controls not only tell the project team when deviations from the plan occur, but also measure progress towards the project's goal. Supporting processes include scope control, change control, schedule control, budget control, quality control, and a communications plan. The emphasis on controlling processes will occur during the execution and control phase of the project methodology.

CLOSING PHASE

The closing process focuses on bringing a project to a systematic and orderly completion. The project team must verify that all deliverables have been satisfactorily completed before the project sponsor accepts the project's product. In addition, the final product, the information system must be integrated successfully into the day-to-day operations of the organization. Closure of a project should include contract closure and administrative closure. Contract closure ensures that all of the deliverables and agreed-upon terms of the project have been completed and delivered so that the project can end. It allows resources to be reassigned and settlement or payment of any account, if applicable. Administrative closure, on the other hand, involves documenting and archiving all project documents. It also includes evaluating the project in terms of whether it achieved its outcomes. Lessons learned should be documented and stored in a way that allows them to be made available to other project teams, present and future. Although each phase must include closing processes, the major emphasis on closing processes will occur during the close project phase of the project methodology.

MOVING THROUGH PROJECT PHASES

A project is an uncertain business; the larger the project, the more uncertainty. It's for this reason, among others, that projects are broken down into smaller, more manageable phases. A project phase allows a project manager to see the project as a whole and yet still focus on completing the project one phase at a time.

Projects are temporary endeavors to create a unique product or service. All projects must have an end date. Between the project launch and the coveted end date, a project will pass through multiple phases. Consider a project to create a new electronic gadget. This gadget will have several phases to complete from concept to completion: product description, prototype, revision, testing, and so on. The completion of each phase brings the project closer to completion.

Think of any project you may have worked on: a technology rollout, constructing a building, or integrating a new service into a business. Each of these projects will have logical phases that move the project from concept to completion. The sum of the project phases comprises the project life cycle. A project life cycle is the duration of a project. Consider our project to create a new electronic gadget. Once the gadget is completed, has passed testing and regulations, the project doesn't continue-it's done. The life of the project is over and the goal of the project, to create a unique product in this case, has been met. There's no reason for the project to keep going-so its life cycle is over.

PROJECT PHASE DELIVERABLES

Every phase has deliverables. It's one of the main points of having phases. For example, your manager gives you a project that will require four years to complete and has a hefty budget of $122 million. Do you think management is going to say, 'Have fun-see you in four years?'

Of course, in most organizations, that's not going to happen. Management wants to see proof of progress, evidence of work completed, and good news about how well the project is moving. Phases are an ideal method of keeping management informed of the project's progression. The following illustration depicts a project moving from conception to completion. At the end of each phase there is some deliverable that the project manager can show to management and customers. They'll want a schedule of when we'll be spending their money and what they'll be getting in return. And when will this fun happen? At the end of a project phase.

The project manager will be accountable for several things at the end of a project phase:

- The performance of the project to date
- The performance of the project team to date
- Proof of deliverables in the project phase
- Verification of deliverables in alignment with the project scope

STAGE GATES

Project phases are also known as stage gates. Stage gates are used often in manufacturing and product development. A stage gate allows a project to continue after the performance and deliverable review against a set of predefined metrics. If the deliverables of the phase, or stage, met the predefined metrics, the project is allowed to continue. Should the deliverable not meet the metrics, the project may not be allowed to pass through the gate to move forward. In these unfortunate cases, the project may be terminated or sent through revisions to meet the predetermined metrics. The following illustration shows the advancement of the project through phases.

The completion of a phase may also be known as a phase exit. A phase exit requires the project deliverable to meet some predetermined exit criteria. Exit criteria are typically inspection-specific and are scheduled events in the project schedule. Exit criteria can include many different activities, such as:

- Sign-offs from the customer
- Regulatory inspections and audits
- Quality metrics
- Performance metrics
- Security audits

Project life cycles, comprised of phases, move the project along. Project life cycles allow a project manager to determine several things about the project, such as:

- What work will be completed in each phase of the project?
- What resources, people, equipment, and facilities will be needed within each phase?
- What are the expected deliverables of each phase?
- What is the expected cost to complete a project phase?
- Which phases contain the highest amount of risk?

Armed with the appropriate information for each project phase, the project manager can plan for cost, schedules, resource availability, risk management, and other project management activities to ensure that the project progresses successfully.

Chapter 8 : PROJECT GOVERNANCE AND STAKEHOLDERS

PROJECT SPONSOR

The project sponsor is a manager with a demonstrable interest in the outcome of the project who is responsible for securing spending authority and resources for the project. Ideally, the project sponsor should be the highest-ranking manager possible, in proportion to the project size and scope. The project sponsor initiates the project proposal process, champions the project in the customer organization, and is the ultimate decision-maker for the project. The project sponsor provides support for the Engineering Manager, approves major deliverables, and signs off on approvals to proceed to each succeeding project phase. The project sponsor may elect to delegate any of the above responsibilities to other personnel either on or outside the project team.

The project sponsor has ultimate accountability and responsibility for the project and is a member of the steering committee, usually the committee chair (sometimes referred to as the project owner). The sponsor oversees the business management and project management issues that arise outside the formal business of the steering committee. The sponsor also lends support, by advocacy, at senior levels, and ensures that the necessary resources (both financial and human) are available to the project.

The corporate client and project sponsor may be the same person for some projects. The project sponsor is ultimately responsible for ensuring that project benefits are secured before formally closing the project. The project sponsor must be identified for all projects, no matter what the size or complexity.

CUSTOMER ORGANIZATION MANAGEMENT

Customer organization management includes all members of the organization's management team that may exert influence on project team members or be affected by and involved in the development and implementation of the product of the project. The committees that are formed to evaluate and select proposed projects for the customer organization are comprised of members of the customer organization management.

STEERING COMMITTEE

The steering committee is responsible for policy and resourcing decisions essential to the delivery of project outputs and the attainment of project target outcomes. It is also responsible for ensuring appropriate management of the project components outlined in the project business plan, including ultimate accountability for ensuring appropriate risk management processes are applied.

INTERNAL STAKEHOLDERS

Internal stakeholders include all the people that are in any way affected by the new product or service within the customer organization. This may include the project team, the customer organization management, customers who will be affected by the change in customer work practices due to the new product or service. External stakeholders include all the people outside the customer organization that are in any way affected by the new product or service.

CUSTOMER

Customer comprise the business units that identified the need for the product or service the project will develop. Customers can be at all levels of an organization, from commissioner to entry-level clerk.

Customer Representatives

Customer representatives are members of the customer community that are identified and made available to the project for their subject matter expertise. Their responsibility is to accurately represent their business units' needs to the project team, and to validate the deliverables that describe the product or service that the project will produce.

Consumers

Consumers include all the people that will use the product or service that the project is developing. Consumers internal to the customer organizations may also be customers.

Business Owner

The business owner is responsible for managing the project outputs for utilization by the project customers. There may be one or more business owners, at a number of managerial levels, depending on the size of the project. The business owner must be satisfied that the project includes all of the outputs necessary for outcome/benefits realization. The business owner must be identified for all projects, no matter what the size or complexity.

Quality Consultant

Large projects generally engage one or more quality consultants to undertake formal quality reviews of the project's processes or outputs. These consultants work independently of the project team, and are often contracted from outside the organization.

Engineering Manager

The Engineering Manager is the person who is responsible for ensuring that the project team completes the project. The Engineering Manager develops the project plan with the team and manages the team's performance of project tasks. It is also the responsibility of the Engineering Manager to secure acceptance and approval of deliverables from the project sponsor and stakeholders.

The Engineering Manager is contracted by the project sponsor and steering committee to deliver the defined project outputs. They are responsible for organizing the project into one or more sub-projects, managing the day-to-day aspects of the project, developing the project management plan, resolving planning and implementation issues, and monitoring progress and budget.

The Engineering Manager will:

- develop and maintain a project management plan
- manage and monitor the project activity through detailed plans and schedules
- report to the project sponsor and steering committee at regular intervals
- manage (client/provider/stakeholder) expectations through formal specification and agreement of goals, objectives, scope, outputs, resources required, budget, schedule, project structure, roles and responsibilities.

It is essential that the Engineering Manager has sound project management skills. An Engineering Manager cannot lead effectively unless they have credibility. For most projects, it means the Engineering Manager must have knowledge of how the outputs will be created and how they will achieve the outcomes or benefits. The Engineering Manager must be identified for all projects, no matter what the size or complexity.

PROJECT TEAM

The project team is a group that is responsible for planning and executing the project. It consists of an Engineering Manager and a variable number of project team members, who are brought in to deliver their tasks according to the project schedule.

The project team is led by the Engineering Manager, working for the successful delivery of the project outputs, as outlined in the project execution plan. It is desirable that the project team includes representatives from the business units affected by the project. The composition of the team may change as the project moves through its various phases. The assessment and selection of people with the requisite skills required for each phase of a project is critical to its overall success. The skills should be explicitly identified as a part of the project planning process. The project team is responsible for completing tasks and activities required for delivering project outputs.

Project Team Members

Project team members are responsible for executing tasks and producing deliverables as outlined in the project management plan and directed by the Engineering Manager, at whatever level of effort or participation has been defined for them. On larger projects, some project team members may serve as team leaders, providing task and technical leadership.

Engineering Consultants

Engineering Consultants are employed from outside the organization to provide specialist or other expertise unavailable from internal resources. Typically, project consultants may include:

- Engineering specialists who define and manage the technological aspects of the project
- representatives employed by stakeholders to ensure their interests are represented and managed
- legal advisers who assist in the development and review of the contractual documentation

ENGINEERING CONTRACTORS

Engineering Contractors also may be engaged to work as part of the project team. Contractors are employed, external to the business area, to provide a specified service in relation to the development of project outputs.

Examples include:
- prepare and deliver training to staff in the business area
- develop and deliver marketing programs
- develop guides and/or manuals
- develop business application software

VENDORS

Vendors are contracted to provide additional products or services the project will require and may be members of the project team.

STEERING COMMITTEE ROLES AND FUNCTIONS

Steering Committee is crucial for the project's success. The important role that Steering Committee members play in a project, both individually and collectively.

The primary function of a Steering Committee is to take responsibility for the business issues associated with a project, including ultimate responsibility for ensuring appropriate risk management processes are applied. Members of a Steering Committee ensure these issues are being adequately addressed and the project remains under control. In practice, these responsibilities involve five main functions:

- Approval of changes to the project and its supporting documentation
- Monitoring and review of the project
- Assistance to the project when required

- Resolution of project conflicts
- Formal acceptance of project deliverables

APPROVAL OF CHANGES TO THE PROJECT

The Steering Committee is responsible for approving major project documentation. Specifically, the Steering Committee approves:
- Prioritization of project objectives and outcomes/benefits
- Budget
- Outputs or deliverables
- Schedule and budget constraints
- Risk minimization strategies
- Project management and quality assurance methodologies

The Steering Committee is also responsible for any major changes to the project. It should be provided with the following information in support of a proposed change:
- Nature and reason for the variation
- Effect of the change
- Revised Project Business Plan, if appropriate
- Suggested actions for the Steering Committee to consider

Changing or emergent issues may require the project scope to be adapted so the project meets the original or modified outcomes/benefits. The Steering Committee is responsible for approving or rejecting these changes to the project and for ensuring that additional resources are provided for incorporating these changes, if required.

MONITORING AND REVIEW OF THE PROJECT

The Steering Committee reviews the status of the project at least at the end of each phase and determines whether the Project Team should progress to the next phase. The review focuses on major project documentation and any variations in the key components, such as outcomes/benefits, risk, costs, returns and output quality.

ASSISTANCE TO THE PROJECT WHEN REQUIRED

The Steering Committee assists the Business Owners and Engineering Manager in completing the project by ensuring the project is adequately resourced and has the backing of people with authority. Steering Committee members should be active advocates for the project's outcomes/benefits and help facilitate broad support for it.

RESOLUTION OF PROJECT CONFLICTS

Project conflicts can arise from conflicts in resource allocation, output quality and the level of commitment of project stakeholders and related projects. The Engineering Manager is generally the first reference point for the resolution of problems and can solve most internal project problems. Problems arising, which are outside the control of the Engineering Manager, are referred to the Project Sponsor or Business Owners for resolution, but there may be occasions when the Steering Committee is asked to help resolve such disputes.

FORMAL ACCEPTANCE OF PROJECT DELIVERABLES

Following review and/or acceptance by the Business Owners, the Steering Committee formally reviews and accepts project outputs. Once these deliverables have been accepted by the Steering Committee, any changes must be formally approved. To achieve this function effectively, Steering Committee members must have a broad understanding of project management concepts and the specific approach adopted by the Project Team.

STEERING COMMITTEE MEMBERSHIP

For Steering Committees to work effectively, the right people must be involved. Steering Committee membership should be based on individual skills and attributes, rather than on their formal roles, and members should maintain membership of a Steering Committee even if their role within the organization changes. However, representatives of important stakeholder groups also should be included.

STEERING COMMITTEE MEETINGS

A Steering Committee meets regularly throughout the course of a project to keep track of issues and the progress of the project. The Engineering Manager should attend these meetings to be a source of information for Steering Committee members and to be kept informed of Steering Committee decisions. Ideally, the Project Sponsor should chair the Steering Committee meetings.

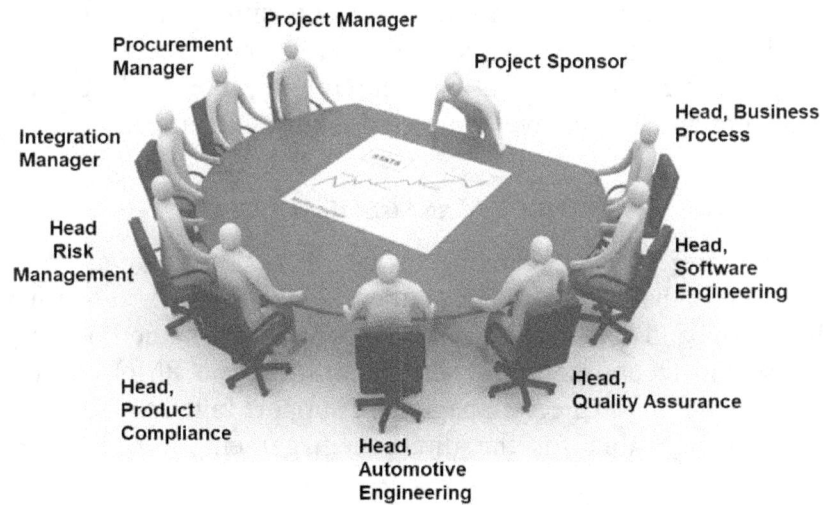

A Steering Committee meeting may cover the following agenda. Introductory items, such as:

- Apologies
- Minutes from last meeting
- Matters arising from minutes
- Project Business Plan issues - amendments, revisions or arising related issues
- Project management issues, including progress reports and consultants' reports
- Important issues at the time of the meeting, such as a budget committee submission, proposed tendering arrangements, sign-off of functional requirements, related projects and so forth
- Review of actions arising from previous Steering Committee meetings - may be useful to keep a formal list of these actions, in order to track them effectively
- Plans for the next meeting

The Steering Committee has responsibility for the project until the project's outcomes/benefits are secured. These outcomes/benefits may not be secured until after the Engineering Manager and Team have completed their involvement.

PROJECT MANAGEMENT OFFICE

A project management office (PMO) is a management structure that standardizes the project-related governance processes and facilitates the sharing of resources, methodologies, tools, and techniques. The responsibilities of a PMO can range from providing project management support functions to actually being responsible for the direct management of one or more projects.

There are several types of PMO structures in organizations, each varying in the degree of control and influence they have on projects within the organization, such as:

- **Supportive**. Supportive PMOs provide a consultative role to projects by supplying templates, best practices, training, access to information and lessons learned from other projects. This type of PMO serves as a project repository. The degree of control provided by the PMO is low.
- **Controlling**. Controlling PMOs provide support and require compliance through various means. Compliance may involve adopting project management frameworks or methodologies, using specific templates, forms and tools, or conformance to governance. The degree of control provided by the PMO is moderate.
- **Directive**. Directive PMOs take control of the projects by directly managing the projects. The degree of control provided by the PMO is high.

A primary function of a PMO is to support Engineering Managers in a variety of ways which may include, but are not limited to:

- Managing shared resources across all projects administered by the PMO;
- Identifying and developing project management methodology, best practices, and standards;
- Coaching, mentoring, training, and oversight;
- Monitoring compliance with project management standards, policies, procedures, and templates by means of project audits;
- Developing and managing project policies, procedures, templates, and other shared documentation (organizational process assets); and
- Coordinating communication across projects.

The key ingredients to project management are people, processes, and technology. Technology is a tool, while processes provide a structure and path for managing and carrying out the project. The success of a project, however, is often determined by the various project stakeholders, as well as who is (or who is not) on the project team. In this chapter, we will discuss the human resources of project management. The area of project human resource management entails:

- organizational planning
- staff acquisition
- team development

Organization planning focuses on the roles, responsibilities, and relationships among the project stakeholders. These individuals or groups can be internal or external to the project. Moreover, organizational planning involves creating a project structure that will support the project processes and stakeholders so that the project is carried out efficiently and effectively.

Staff acquisition includes staffing the project with the best available human resources. Effective staffing involves having policies, procedures, and practices to guide the recruitment of appropriately skilled and experienced staff. Moreover, it may include negotiating for staff from other functional areas within the organization.

Team development involves creating an environment to develop and support the individual team members and the team itself.

This chapter will expand upon these three subjects and integrate several relatively recent concepts for understanding the governance structure in project management. Three primary organizational structure: the functional, project, and matrix will be described. In addition, the various opportunities and challenges for projects conducted under each structure will be discussed. As a project manager or project team member, it is important to understand an organization's structure since this will determine authorities, roles, responsibilities, communication channels, and availability of resources.

Once the project team is in place, it is important that the project team learn from each other and from past project experiences. Thus, the idea of learning cycles will be introduced as a tool for team learning and for capturing lessons learned that can be documented, stored, and retrieved using a knowledge management system

PROJECT STAKEHOLDERS

Stakeholders are individuals, groups, or even organizations that have a stake, or claim, in the project's outcome. Often, we think of stakeholders as only those individuals or groups having an interest in the successful outcome of a project, but the sad truth is that there are many who can gain from a project's failure. While the formal organization tells us a little about the stakeholders and what their interests may be, the informal organization paints a much more interesting picture.

Types of Stakeholders in Project Management

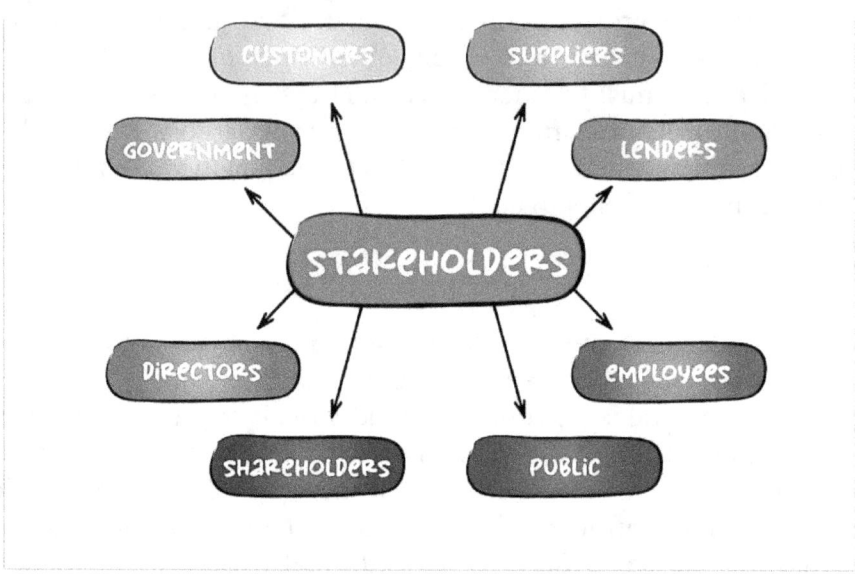

PROJECT MANAGER

One of the most critical decisions in project management is selecting a project manager or team leader. The project manager is usually assigned to the project at the earliest stages of the project life cycle, but a new one may be brought in as replacement in the later stages of a project. The project manager must play many roles. First, the project manager must play a managerial role that focuses on planning, organizing, and controlling. The project manager, for example, is responsible for developing the project plan, organizing the project resources, and then overseeing execution of the plan. The project manager must also perform many administrative functions, including performance reviews, project tracking and reporting, and other general day-to-day responsibilities.

The success of the project, of course, depends not only on the project team, but also on the contributions and support of all project stakeholders as well. Therefore, the project manager must build and nurture the relationships among the various stakeholders. To do this effectively, the project manager must play a strong leadership role. While the managerial role focuses on planning, organizing, and controlling, leadership focuses on getting people motivated and then headed down the right path towards a common goal.

Choosing a project manager for a project is analogous to hiring an employee. It is important to look at his or her background, knowledge, skill sets, and overall strengths and weaknesses. Some attributes of a successful project manager include:

ABILITY TO COMMUNICATE WITH PEOPLE

A project manager must have strong communication skills. A project manager need not to be a great motivational speaker, but should have the ability to connect with people, share a common vision, and get everyone to respond or head in the right direction.

ABILITY TO DEAL WITH PEOPLE

Aside from being a good communicator, a project manager must have the soft skills for dealing with people, their egos, and their agendas. The project manager must be a good listener, hearing what people say and understanding what they mean. This skill allows the project manager to get below the surface of issues when people are not being completely honest or open without being annoying or alienating them.

ABILITY TO CREATE AND SUSTAIN RELATIONSHIPS

A good project manager must be able to build bridges instead of walls. Acting as a peacemaker or negotiator among the project client or sponsor, top management, the project team, customers, suppliers, vendors, subcontractors, and so forth may be necessary.

ABILITY TO ORGANIZE

A project manager must be good at organizing developing the project plan, acquiring resources, and creating an effective project environment. The project manager must also know and understand both the details and the big picture, which requires a familiarity with the details of the project plan and also an understanding of how contingencies may impact the plan.

The following list of project roles gives an indication of the type of accountabilities, responsibilities and tasks generally allocated to those people involved in a project. As projects vary, including in size and complexity, the roles required, and even the tasks and responsibilities within those roles, will vary. The information below provides a starting point, which should be discussed with the appropriate groups or persons nominated to fill positions in a project's governance structure, with the agreed breakdown of accountabilities and responsibilities documented for large and/or complex projects. The most crucial issue is to have clearly assigned roles and transparency of the project governance structure.

However, all projects must have, as a minimum, the roles of Project Sponsor, Business Owner(s) and Project Manager within the governance structure (though not necessarily different person). That is:

- A person responsible and accountable for the project output and securing its benefits (Project Sponsor)
- A person who will manage the project outputs after project closure, and is accountable for realization of the benefits (Business Owners)
- A person who will manage the project and deliver the outputs (Project Manager)

Budget Management

Project Manager must be capable to prepare the project budget. All businesses have a responsibility to the monies they are allotted, have earned, and have acquired through donations. In project management, the work completed within a project must be measured for value and accounted for. The budget the organization has set for the project must be guarded. Ultimately, the success of the project should generate an increase in funds, productivity, or efficiency for the sponsoring organization.

Project Resources

Project Manager must be organized. How much time has been wasted looking for documentation, contracts, or permits? How much money has been lost due to disorganization? How many projects have failed because the project manager did not keep and maintain accurate records? Organization is a methodical approach to storing and retrieving information, as it is needed. Organization does not require a spotless desk, thousands of labelled file folders, or archives of every project-related document. Organization requires thorough, fast, and reliable access to project data.

Project Sponsor

The project sponsor is a manager with demonstrable interest in the outcome of the project who is responsible for securing spending authority and resources for the project. Ideally, the project sponsor should be the highest-ranking manager possible, in proportion to the project size and scope. The project sponsor initiates the project proposal process, champions the project in the customer organization, and is the ultimate decision-maker for the project. The project sponsor provides support for the project manager, approves major deliverables, and signs off on approvals to proceed to each succeeding project phase. The project sponsor may elect to delegate any of the above responsibilities to other personnel either on or outside the project team.

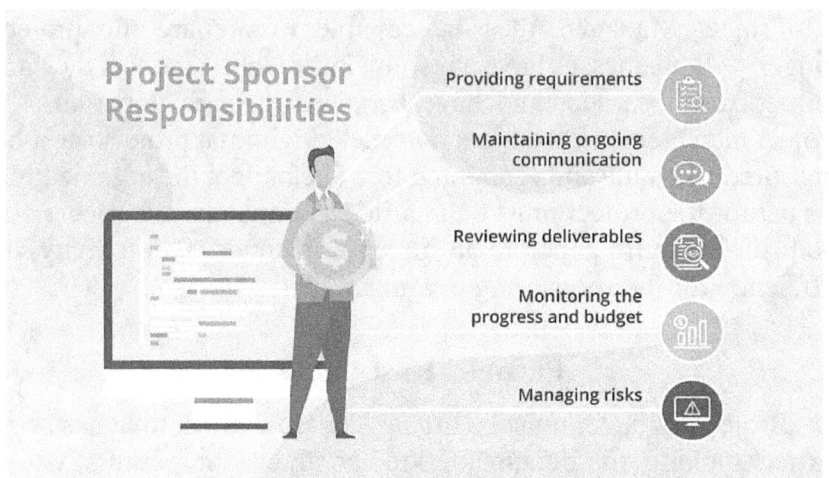

The project sponsor has ultimate accountability and responsibility for the project and is a member of the steering committee, usually the committee chair (sometimes referred to as project owner). The sponsor oversees the business management and project management issues that arise outside the formal business of the steering committee. The sponsor also lends support, by advocacy, at senior levels, and ensures that the necessary resources (both financial and human) are available to the project.

The corporate client and project sponsor may be the same person for some projects. The project sponsor is ultimately responsible for ensuring that project benefits are secured before formally closing the project. The project sponsor must be identified for all projects, no matter what the size or complexity.

CUSTOMER ORGANIZATION MANAGEMENT

Customer organization management (pom) includes all members of the organization's management team that may exert influence on project team members or be affected by and involved in the development and implementation of the product of the project. The committees that are formed to evaluate and select proposed projects for the customer organization are comprised of members of the customer organization management.

PROJECT STEERING COMMITTEE

The steering committee is responsible for policy and resourcing decisions essential to delivery of project outputs and the attainment of project target outcomes. It is also responsible for ensuring appropriate management of the project components outlined in the project business plan, including ultimate accountability for ensuring appropriate risk management processes are applied.

PROJECT STAKEHOLDERS

Internal stakeholders include all the people that are in any way affected by the new product or service within the customer organization. This may include the project team, the customer organization management, customers who will be affected by the change in customer work practices due to the new product or service. External stakeholders include all the people outside the customer organization that are in any way affected by the new product or service.

CUSTOMER

Customer comprise the business units that identified the need for the product or service the project will develop. Customers can be at all levels of an organization, from commissioner to entry-level clerk.

CUSTOMER REPRESENTATIVES

Customer representatives are members of the customer community that are identified and made available to the project for their subject matter expertise. Their responsibility is to accurately represent their business units' needs to the project team, and to validate the deliverables that describe the product or service that the project will produce.

CONSUMERS

Consumers include all the people that will use the product or service that the project is developing. Consumers internal to the customer organizations may also be customers.

BUSINESS OWNER

The business owner is responsible for managing the project outputs for utilization by the project customers. There may be one or more business owners, at a number of managerial levels, depending on the size of the project. The business owner must be satisfied that the project includes all of the outputs necessary for outcome/benefits realization. The business owner must be identified for all projects, no matter what the size or complexity.

QUALITY CONSULTANT

Large projects generally engage one or more quality consultants to undertake formal quality reviews of the project's processes or outputs. These consultants work independently of the project team, and are often contracted from outside the organization.

PROJECT MANAGER

The project manager is the person who is responsible for ensuring that the project team completes the project. The project manager develops the project plan with the team and manages the team's performance of project tasks. It is also the responsibility of the project manager to secure acceptance and approval of deliverables from the project sponsor and stakeholders.

The project manager is contracted by the project sponsor and steering committee to deliver the defined project outputs. They are responsible for organizing the project into one or more sub-projects, managing the day-to-day aspects of the project, developing the project management plan, resolving planning and implementation issues, and monitoring progress and budget.

The project manager will:

- develop and maintain a project management plan
- manage and monitor the project activity through detailed plans and schedules
- report to the project sponsor and steering committee at regular intervals
- manage (client/provider/stakeholder) expectations through formal specification and agreement of goals, objectives, scope, outputs, resources required, budget, schedule, project structure, roles and responsibilities.

It is essential that the project manager has high-level project management skills. A project manager cannot lead effectively unless they have credibility. For most projects, it means the project manager must have knowledge of how the outputs will be created and how they will achieve the outcomes or benefits. The project manager must be identified for all projects, no matter what the size or complexity.

PROJECT TEAM

The project team is a group that is responsible for planning and executing the project. It consists of a project manager and a variable number of project team members, who are brought in to deliver their tasks according to the project schedule.

The project team is led by the project manager, working for the successful delivery of the project outputs, as outlined in the project execution plan. It is desirable that the project team includes representatives from the business units affected by the project. The composition of the team may change as the project moves through its various phases. The assessment and selection of people with the requisite skills required for each phase of a project is critical to its overall success. The skills should be explicitly identified as a part of the project planning process. The project team is responsible for completing tasks and activities required for delivering project outputs.

PROJECT TEAM MEMBERS

Project team members are responsible for executing tasks and producing deliverables as outlined in the project management plan and directed by the project manager, at whatever level of effort or participation has been defined for them.

On larger projects, some project team members may serve as team leaders, providing task and technical leadership.

CONSULTANTS

Consultants are employed from outside the organization to provide specialist or other expertise unavailable from internal resources. Typically, project consultants may include:

- engineering specialists who define and manage the technological aspects of the project
- representatives employed by stakeholders to ensure their interests are represented and managed
- legal advisers who assist in the development and review of the contractual documentation

CONTRACTORS

Contractors also may be engaged to work as part of the project team. Contractors are employed, external to the business area, to provide a specified service in relation to the development of project outputs.

Examples include:

- prepare and deliver training to staff in the business area
- develop and deliver marketing programs
- develop guides and/or manuals
- develop business application software

VENDORS

Vendors are contracted to provide additional products or services the project will require and may be members of the project team.

PROJECT STEERING COMMITTEE

Steering Committee is crucial for the project's success. The important role that Steering Committee members play in a project, both individually and collectively.

The primary function of a Steering Committee is to take responsibility for the business issues associated with a project, including ultimate responsibility for ensuring appropriate risk management processes are applied. Members of a Steering Committee ensure these issues are being adequately addressed and the project remains under control. In practice, these responsibilities involve five main functions:

- Approval of changes to the project and its supporting documentation
- Monitoring and review of the project

- Assistance to the project when required
- Resolution of project conflicts
- Formal acceptance of project deliverables

The Steering Committee is responsible for approving major project documentation. Specifically, the Steering Committee approves:

- Prioritization of project objectives and outcomes/benefits
- Budget
- Outputs or deliverables
- Schedule and budget constraints
- Risk minimization strategies
- Project management and quality assurance methodologies

The Steering Committee is also responsible for any major changes to the project. It should be provided with the following information in support of a proposed change:

- Nature and reason for the variation
- Effect of the change
- Revised Project Business Plan, if appropriate
- Suggested actions for the Steering Committee to consider

Changing or emergent issues may require the project scope to be adapted so the project meets the original or modified outcomes/benefits. The Steering Committee is responsible for approving or rejecting these changes to the project and for ensuring that additional resources are provided for incorporating these changes, if required.

MONITORING AND REVIEW

The Steering Committee reviews the status of the project at least at the end of each phase and determines whether the Project Team should progress to the next phase. The review focuses on major project documentation and any variations in the key components, such as outcomes/benefits, risk, costs, returns and output quality.

ASSISTANCE TO THE PROJECT

The Steering Committee assists the Business Owners and Project Manager in completing the project by ensuring the project is adequately resourced and has the backing of people with authority. Steering Committee members should be active advocates for the project's outcomes/benefits and help facilitate broad support for it.

RESOLUTION OF PROJECT CONFLICTS

Project conflicts can arise from conflicts in resource allocation, output quality and the level of commitment of project stakeholders and related projects.

The Project Manager is generally the first reference point for the resolution of problems and can solve most internal project problems. Problems arising, which are outside the control of the Project Manager, are referred to the Project Sponsor or Business Owners for resolution, but there may be occasions when the Steering Committee is asked to help resolve such disputes.

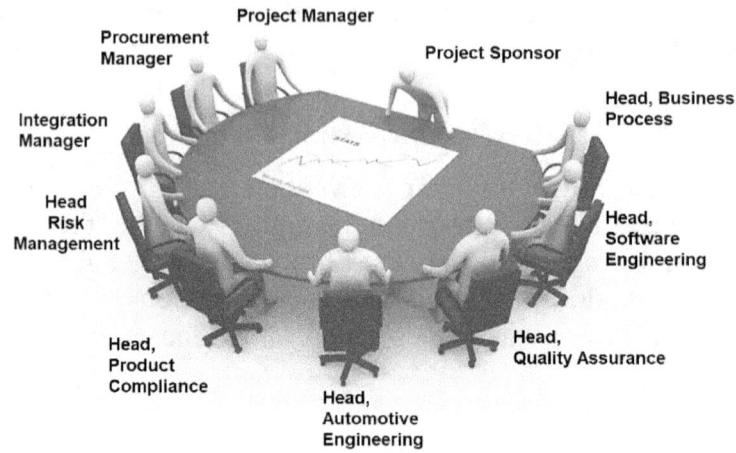

FORMAL ACCEPTANCE OF PROJECT DELIVERABLES

Following review and/or acceptance by the Business Owners, the Steering Committee formally reviews and accepts project outputs. Once these deliverables have been accepted by the Steering Committee, any changes must be formally approved. To achieve this function effectively, Steering Committee members must have a broad understanding of project management concepts and the specific approach adopted by the Project Team.

STEERING COMMITTEE MEMBERSHIP

For Steering Committees to work effectively, the right people must be involved. Steering Committee membership should be based on individual skills and attributes, rather than on their formal roles, and members should maintain membership of a Steering Committee even if their role within the organization changes. However, representatives of important stakeholder groups also should be included.

STEERING COMMITTEE MEETINGS

A Steering Committee meets regularly throughout the course of a project to keep track of issues and the progress of the project. The Project Manager should attend these meetings to be a source of information for Steering Committee members and to be kept informed of Steering Committee decisions. Ideally, the Project Sponsor should chair the Steering Committee meetings. A Steering Committee meeting may cover the following agenda:

- Apologies
- Minutes from last meeting
- Matters arising from minutes
- Project Business Plan issues - amendments, revisions or arising related issues
- Project management issues, including progress reports and consultants' reports
- Important issues at the time of the meeting, such as a budget committee submission, proposed tendering arrangements, sign-off of functional requirements, related projects and so forth
- Review of actions arising from previous Steering Committee meetings - may be useful to keep a formal list of these actions, in order to track them effectively
- Plans for the next meeting

The Steering Committee has responsibility for the project until the project's outcomes/benefits are secured. These outcomes/benefits may not be secured until after the Project Manager and Team have completed their involvement.

Project Management Office

A project management office (PMO) is a management structure that standardizes the project-related governance processes and facilitates the sharing of resources, methodologies, tools, and techniques. The responsibilities of a PMO can range from providing project management support functions to actually being responsible for the direct management of one or more projects.

There are several types of PMO structures in organizations, each varying in the degree of control and influence they have on projects within the organization, such as:

- **Supportive.** Supportive PMOs provide a consultative role to projects by supplying templates, best practices, training, access to information and lessons learned from other projects. This type of PMO serves as a project repository. The degree of control provided by the PMO is low.
- **Controlling.** Controlling PMOs provide support and require compliance through various means. Compliance may involve adopting project management frameworks or methodologies, using specific templates, forms and tools, or conformance to governance. The degree of control provided by the PMO is moderate.
- **Directive.** Directive PMOs take control of the projects by directly managing the projects. The degree of control provided by the PMO is high.

A primary function of a PMO is to support project managers in a variety of ways which may include, but are not limited to:

- Managing shared resources across all projects administered by the PMO;
- Identifying and developing project management methodology, best practices, and standards;

- Coaching, mentoring, training, and oversight;
- Monitoring compliance with project management standards, policies, procedures, and templates by means of project audits;
- Developing and managing project policies, procedures, templates, and other shared documentation (organizational process assets); and
- Coordinating communication across projects.

Chapter 9 :   RISK MANAGEMENT

All businesses exist for one clear reason: to make a profit. Risk is embedded in every opportunity a business face. Poorly managed risks have tangible and dramatic effects. Sound risk management is important to ensure that the business can overcome any problems and continue to grow profitably. This will result in a great return on investment. Project risk management is a facet of quality, using basic techniques of analysis and measurement to ensure that risks are properly identified, classified and managed. An organisation can compete well in terms of its resources, earnings and cash flows if an efficient pre-loss plan that minimises the adverse impact of risk is managed well.

They will always welcome reengineering and process improvement. The purpose of project risk management is to maximise the results of positive events and minimise the results of adverse events. In order to achieve the abovementioned benefits, project risk management requires staff that can play these roles professionally to achieve improved project success.

By now, you are already familiar with the concept of a project life cycle. Let's take closer look at the pattern of risks in the life of a project.

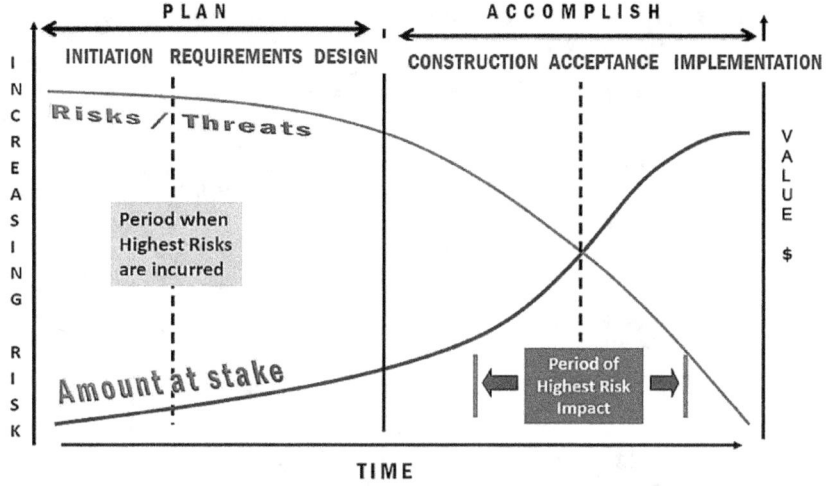

RISKS ARE AT ITS PEAK AT BEGINNING OF PROJECT, INVESTMENT IS LOW

Risks are highest during project initiation because known and unknown threats are likely to hit the project. At this stage the project manager has completed definition of some risks based on input from project business case. A Risk Register will be created to record these risks, you will need them later during project planning.

Risks are at its Peak during initiating the project ; Investment is Low
- Risks are highest during initiation because known and unknown threats are likely to hit the project.
- Investment is low since the only minimum number of resources are required at this stage.
- The primary work focus is to develop the initial project plan, preliminary budget, defining the scope, and to develop a high level project schedule.

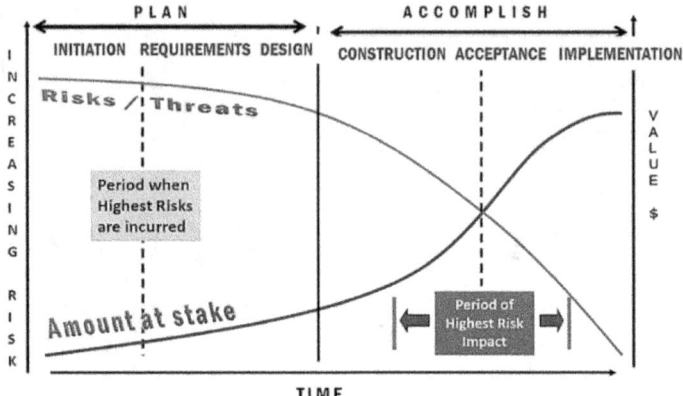

Investment is low since only minimum number of resources are required at this stage. You will have few people in your team to start developing the initial project plan, preliminary budget, defining project scope, and to develop a high-level project schedule.

INVESTMENT INCREASES DURING PLANNING PHASE, MAJOR RISKS IDENTIFIED

In planning the project, the project manager has verified the high priority risks defined in the risk register. These risks will be analyzed using qualitative and quantitative methods and prioritized according to their severity level. Investment increases due to engagement of human resources to develop the Project Team and to produce the project management plan, risk management plan, and communications plan, and many other project subsidiary plans. Project budget and project schedule will be finalized to produce the project baseline.

Risks are at its Peak during initiating the project ; Investment is Low

- Risks are highest during initiation because known and unknown threats are likely to hit the project.
- Investment is low since the only minimum number of resources are required at this stage.
- The primary work focus is to develop the initial project plan, preliminary budget, defining the scope, and to develop a high level project schedule.

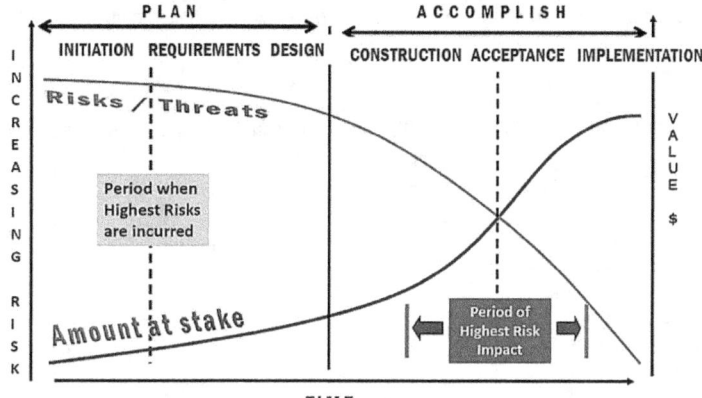

BUDGETS UTILIZED DURING PROJECT EXECUTION PHASE

Budget utilized during Construction phase; Risks tracking in progress
- Investment increases due to the procurement of materials, and more people are joining the project to assist in development and testing activities.
- High impact risks that may impact development work and testing are closely monitored

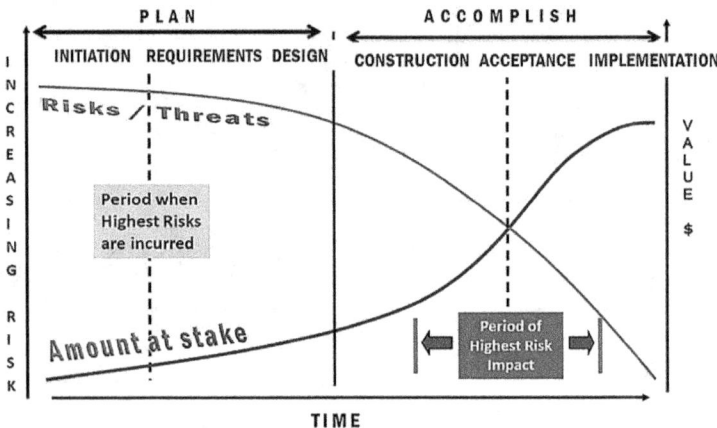

Investment increases due to procurement of materials, and more people are joining the project team to assist in development and testing activities. Risk events classified as critical risks that may impact development work and testing are closely monitored. At this stage the project manager needs to manage scope changes, manage risks, manage issues, and manage the project team to ensure that the development work runs according to the project plan.

HIGHEST RISK IMPACT AT THE CLOSING STAGE OF PROJECT

Impact of risks will be felt the most during the project control phase where the scope of the product is verified against the product requirements. Customers will perform the product verification following the acceptance management process defined during project planning. If product verification failed, the project schedule will be extended, and project budget will certainly increase. This is the period of highest risk impact because it determines whether the project meet the objectives specified in the project charter.

Highest risk impact at the Acceptance phase.
- Impact of risks will be felt the most during the acceptance management process where the scope of the product is measured against the product requirements.
- If product verification failed, the project schedule will be extended, project cost will increase.

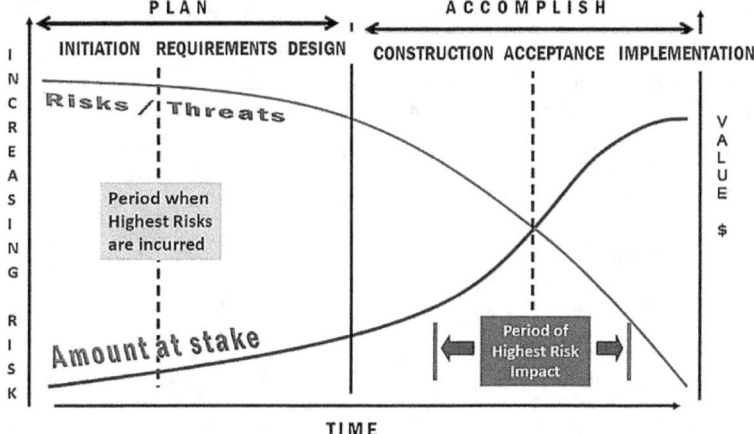

RISKS HAVE BEEN TREATED AND PROJECT DELIVERABLES ACCEPTED

During Implementation phase, risks have been treated, Project deliverables are accepted, Project delivered within budget, scope, schedule, and quality.

The project delivers value to the organization when the project output ("product" or "services") meet the requirements defined in the project charter.

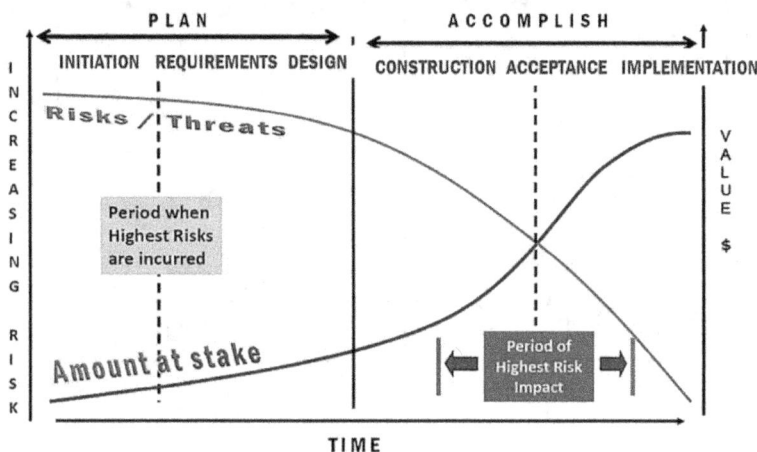

At the closing phase of the project life cycle, all major risks affecting the project have been treated, some may have been treated by executing the mitigation plans, while others may be subject to risk contingency actions. The project performance being measured against the project baselines defined during project planning. The project delivers value to the organization when the project output ("product" or "services") meets the requirements defined in the project charter, and also the project meets the budget, scope, schedule, and quality requirements.

RISK AFFECTING PROJECT CONSTRAINTS

Project constraints influence practically all areas of the project process. Consider constraints as a ruling requirement over the project. Common constraints you'll encounter are time constraints in the form of deadlines and the availability of resources.

Specifically, there are four major constraints that a project manager encounter, they are Scope, Schedule, Cost, and Quality. A project manager will have to deal with several threats during execution of the project activities where these threats are most likely going to affect the time taken to deliver the project; it may affect the original budget that was agreed during project planning; or it may affect the scope and quality of the finished product.

Every project has some degree of risks. Risk items come up on every project. Recognizing issues as Risks when they arise is a talent and it's one that the Project Manager and the delivery team need to acquire to help ensure project success. Sometimes it requires out-of-the-box thinking and not just basing everything on the fact that it's "never happened that way before." That's a dangerous mentality. Check for risks throughout the project and keep revisiting the list of risks that have been identified to ensure that they are planned for in the event that they are realized during the lifetime of the project.

Identification, analysis, measurement and management of risk, requires specialized knowledge and skill. Engineering risk management has to be done in every organization, and every organization has its own unique engineering risk profile. engineering risks can be classified according to their impact on the organisation7, as follows:

- security risk
- availability risk
- performance risk
- compliance risk

Security Risk

The information will be altered, accessed, or used by unauthorized parties. Sources of security risk could be: external attacks, malicious code, physical destruction, inappropriate access, unsatisfied employees, variety of platform and messaging types. Potential impacts associated with them are: corruption of information, external fraud, identity theft, theft of financial assets, damage to reputation and damage to assets.

Availability Risk

Availability risk that information or applications will be inaccessible due to system failure or natural disaster, including any recovery period. Sources of availability risk are: hardware failures, network outages, data center failures, force majeure. Potential impacts associated with them are: abandoned transactions and lost sales, reduced customer, partner, or employee confidence, interruption or delay of business-critical processes, reduced engineering staff productivity.

Performance Risk

Performance risk refer to underperformance of systems, applications, or personnel, or engineering as a whole will diminish business productivity or value. Sources of performance risk are: poor system architectures, network congestion, inefficient code, inadequate capacity. Potential impacts associated with them are: reduced client satisfaction and loyalty, interruption or delay of business-critical process, lost engineering productivity.

Compliance Risk

Compliance risk refer to the information handling or processing that will fail to meet regulatory, engineering or business policy requirements. Usually, it involves penalties, fines, or loss of reputation from failure to comply with laws or regulations, or consequences of non-compliance with engineering policies. Sources of compliance risk are: regulations unique to each jurisdiction legal actions, internal engineering safeguards supporting compliance, inadequate third-party compliance standards. Potential impacts associated with them are: damage to reputation, breach of client confidentiality, litigation.

RISK MANAGEMENT PROCESSES

The five processes of enterprise risk management are risk management planning, risk identification, risk assessment, risk response, and risk monitoring and control. These five processes interact with enterprise risk management, project communications management, and project integration management that allow the project manager, project sponsor, and project team, to manage known threats that impact project objectives.

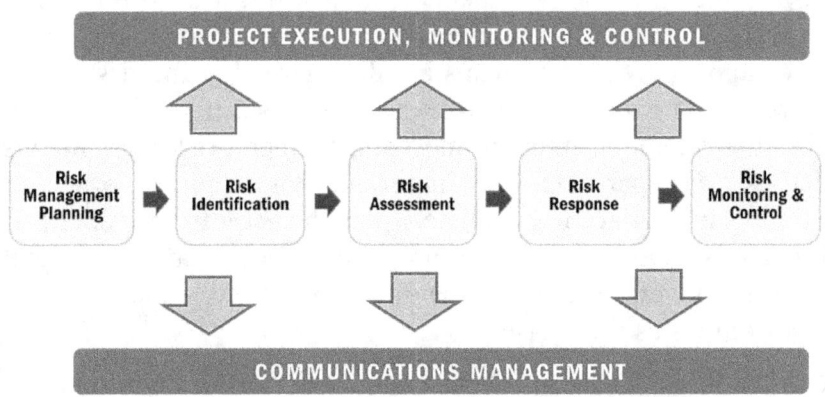

Enterprise risk management is the systematic process of identifying, analyzing, and responding to project risk. It includes maximizing the probability and consequences of positive events and minimizing the probability and consequences of adverse events.

There are five key processes associated with enterprise risk management.

- Risk Management Planning

- Risk Identification
- Risk Assessment
- Risk Response
- Risk Monitoring and Control

RISK MANAGEMENT PLANNING

Risk management planning is the first step and begins with having a firm commitment to the entire risk management approach from all project stakeholders. This commitment ensures that adequate resources will be in place to properly plan for and manage the various risks of the project. These resources may include time, people, and technology. Stakeholders also must be committed to the process of identifying, analyzing, and responding to threats and opportunities. Too often plans are disregarded at the first sign of trouble, and instinctive reactions to situations can lead to perpetual crisis management. In addition to commitment, risk planning also focuses on preparation. It is important that resources, processes, and tools be in place to adequately plan the activities for enterprise risk management. Systematic preparation and planning can help minimize adverse effects on the project while taking advantage of opportunities as they arise.

The Risk Management Plan is responsible for determining:

- How risks will be identified
- How quantitative analysis will be completed
- How qualitative analysis will be completed
- How risk response planning will happen
- How risks will be monitored
- What an ongoing risk management activity will happen throughout the project life cycle

WHY WOULD YOU DEVELOP THE ENTERPRISE RISK MANAGEMENT PLAN?

A Risk Management Plan is developed:

- To ensure levels of risk and uncertainty are properly managed so that the project is successfully completed.
- To provide a useful tool for managing and reducing the risks identified before and during the project
- To document risk mitigation strategies being pursued in response to the identified risks and their grading in terms of likelihood and impact
- To provide the Project Sponsor, Steering Committee/senior management with a documented framework from which risk status can be reported upon
- To document the process that will be adopted by the project to identify, analyse and evaluate risks during the remainder of the project.
- To define how risk mitigation strategies will be developed and deployed to reduce the likelihood impact of risks.
- To determine how often risks will be reviewed, the process for review and who will be involved.
- To establish roles and responsibilities for risk management
- To decide how reporting on risk status, and changes to risk status, will be undertaken within the Project and to the Steering Committee
- To produce a complete Risk Register containing all risks identified for the Project, their current grading and the identified risk mitigation strategies to reduce the likelihood and seriousness of each risk.
- To ensure the communication of risk management issues to key stakeholders

- To provide a mechanism for seeking and acting on feedback and encourage the involvement of the key stakeholders

CONTENT OF THE ENTERPRISE RISK MANAGEMENT PLAN

Purpose

The Risk Management Plan lays down the groundwork for how risk management will be carried out in a project. It serves as guidance for the risk process, its thresholds, and its formats, defining the roles and responsibilities of stakeholders in risk management. It is notable that the Risk Management Plan is not a listing of specific risks and is not used to establish the particular strategies for risks, once they are identified.

Application

The Risk Management Plan is shared with project stakeholders to clarify their roles and responsibilities in the risk management process and to identify when specific potential risks are truly of concern to the organization. It also outlines the risk budgeting process, detailing how and when risk contingency funds may be allocated and applied.

Content

The Risk Management Plan consists of basic information about how risk management will be conducted during the project. It does not address specific behavior associated with specific risks, but instead forms a framework for the rest of the risk management process. Through planning meetings, the Risk Management Plan is created. Risk management plan templates, performing organization policies, and the risk tolerance level of the stakeholders aid the creation of the risk management plan.

RISK IDENTIFICATION

The first step in risk management is identifying the risks that we will see in our project. These are the things that threaten to stop us from delivering what we have promised on the schedule we promised for the budget we promised. If we were completely certain about everything in the project and how it was going to turn out, we would not have to worry about risk management. From this lack of knowledge of how the project is going to unfold come the problems that we will have to deal with. These are the risks we want to identify. Every practical means must be used to discover the risks that are associated with the project. Meetings must be held throughout the project to discover new risks that have appeared and to dismiss risks that can no longer take place.

- Changes in legal or regulatory environment
- Labor issues, changing owner priorities, country risk, and weather.
- Force majeure risks such as earthquakes, floods, and tsunami

WHAT IS RISK IDENTIFICATION?

Risk identification is the process of identifying the threats and opportunities that could occur during the life of the project along with their associated uncertainties. The life of the project means the complete life cycle of the project, not just the time the project team is in place, the time until the final acceptance by the customer, or even the end of the warranty period. Risks should be considered through the useful life of the product or service that we are providing by doing this project. The risk of corrosion causing a catastrophic product failure during the useful life of a product that we have designed and built should be considered, and corrective action should be taken in accordance with the seriousness of the threat. Risks can be identified in a large number of ways, and all of the productive and economical ways should be employed.

During of procurement of materials, you need to get them insured against damages, late delivery, lost, stolen, et cetera.

Risk Management in the Procurement Process

INPUTS INTO RISK IDENTIFICATION

Project planning outputs: Risk identification requires an understanding of the project's mission, scope, and objectives of the owner, sponsor, or stakeholders. Outputs of other processes should be reviewed to identify possible risks across the entire project. These may include, but are not limited to: the project charter, WBS, product description, schedule and cost estimates, resource plan, procurement plan, and assumption and constraint lists.

Risk Categories

These categories should be well defined and should reflect common sources of risk for the industry or application area. These categories include the following:

- **Technical, quality or performance risks** - such as reliance on unproven or complex technology, unrealistic performance goals, changes to the technology used or to industry standards during the project.

- **Project-management risks** - such as poor allocation of time and resources, inadequate quality of the project plan, poor use of project management disciplines.

- **Organizational risks** - such as cost, time, and scope objectives that are internally inconsistent, lack of prioritization of projects, inadequacy or interruption of funding, and resource conflicts with other projects in the organization.

- **External risks** - such as shifting legal or regulatory environment, labor issues, changing owner priorities, country risk, and weather. Force majeure risks such as earthquakes, floods, and civil unrest generally require disaster recovery actions rather than risk management.

- **Historical information** - information on prior projects may be available from project files or published information through commercial or academic sources.

Methods used in Risk Identification

Documentation reviews - includes a structured review of the project plans and assumptions, both at the total project and detailed scope levels as well as reviews of prior project files and other informational sources.

INFORMATION-GATHERING TECHNIQUES

Brainstorming

Probably the most frequently used risk identification technique. Generally performed by the project team although a multidisciplinary set of experts can also perform this technique. The goal is to obtain a comprehensive list of risks that can be addressed later in the qualitative and quantitative risk analysis processes. Under the leadership of a facilitator, the team generates ideas about project risk. Sources of risk are identified in broad scope, posted, categorized by type of risk, and then the definitions sharpened.

Delphi technique

A means for achieving a consensus of experts on a subject such as project risk. Project risk experts are identified but participate anonymously. A facilitator uses a questionnaire to solicit ideas about the important project risks. The responses are submitted and then circulated to the experts for further comment. Consensus may be reached in a few rounds of this process. This technique helps reduce bias in the data and keeps any person from having undue influence on the outcome.

Interviewing

Risks are identified by interviewing experienced project managers or subject-matter experts. The person in charge of risk identification identifies the appropriate individuals, briefs them on the project, and provides information such as the work breakdown structure and the list of assumptions. The interviewees then identify risks. Strengths, weaknesses, opportunities, and threats (SWOT) analysis. Ensures examination of the project from each of the SWOT perspectives to increase the breadth of the risks considered.

Checklists

Lists based on historical information and knowledge that has been accumulated from previous similar projects and other sources of information. An advantage of using a checklist is that the risk identification is quick and simple. The disadvantage of using a checklist is that building a checklist with every possible risk is impossible, and the user may be limited to the categories that appear on the list.

Assumption's analysis

Every project is conceived and developed based on a set of hypotheses, scenarios, or assumptions. Assumption's analysis is a technique that explores whether or not the assumptions are valid. Identifies project risks from inaccuracy, inconsistency, or incompleteness of assumptions.

Diagramming techniques

Cause-and-effect diagrams (also known as Ishikawa or fishbone diagrams) System or process flow charts, Influence diagrams - a graphical representation of a problem, showing causal influences, time ordering of events, and other relationships among variables and outcomes.

RISK ASSESSMENT

Once the project risks have been identified and their causes and effects understood, the next step requires that we analyze these risks. Answers to two basic questions are required: What is the likelihood of a particular risk occurring? And, what is the impact on the project if it does occur? Risk assessment provides a basis for understanding how to deal with project risks. To answer the two questions, qualitative and quantitative approaches can be used. Several tools and techniques for each approach will be introduced later. Assessing these risks helps the project manager and other stakeholders prioritize and formulate responses to those risks that provide the greatest threat or opportunity to the project. Because there is a cost associated with responding to a particular risk, risk management must function within the constraints of the project's available resources.

The framework introduced in the previous section provides tools for identifying and understanding the nature of risks to projects. The next step requires that those risks be analyzed to determine what threats or opportunities require attention or a response.

Risk analysis and assessment provides a systematic approach for evaluating the risks that the project stakeholders identify. The purpose of risk analysis is to determine each identified risk's probability and impact on the project. Risk assessment, on the other hand, focuses on prioritizing risks so that an effective risk strategy can be formulated. In short, which risks require a response? To a great degree, this will be determined by the project stakeholders' tolerances to risk.

OBJECTIVE OF RISK ASSESSMENT

Risk assessment is the process of evaluating the risks that have been identified and developing the data that will be needed for making decisions as to what should be done about them. Risk management is done from very early in the project until the very end. For this reason, qualitative analysis should be used at some points in the project, and quantitative techniques should be used at other times.

The objective of risk assessment is to establish a way of arranging the risks in the order of importance. In most projects there will not be enough time or money to take action against every risk that is identified.

The severity of the risk is a practical measure for quantifying risks. Severity is a combination of the risk probability and the risk impact. In its simplest form the risks can be ranked as high and low severity or possibly high, medium, and low. At the other extreme, the probability of the risk can be a percentage or a decimal value between zero and one, and the impact can be estimated in dollars. When the impact in dollars and the probability in decimal is multiplied together, the result is the quantitative expected value of the risk.

The purpose of risk analysis is to determine each identified risk's probability and impact on the project. Risk assessment, on the other hand, focuses on prioritizing risks so that an effective risk strategy can be formulated.

In short, which risks require a response? To a great degree, this will be determined by the project stakeholders' tolerances to risk. There are two basic approaches to analyzing and assessing project risk. The first approach is more qualitative in nature because it includes subjective assessments based on experience or intuition. Quantitative analysis, on the other hand, is based on mathematical and statistical techniques. Each approach has its own strengths and weaknesses when dealing with uncertainty, so a combination of qualitative and quantitative methods provides valuable insight when conducting risk analysis and assessment.

QUANTITATIVE RISK ANALYSIS

Quantitative Risk Assessment comes into play when we have the ability to map a dollar amount to a specific risk. For example, if there are 1,000 records of confidential patient data at a medical center residing on a single database. This database is accessed directly by a web server which resides in a semi-trusted or DMZ environment. A compromise of the method in which the web server communicates with the database could result in the exposure of all 1,000 records of patient data. Let us also say that during a Business Impact Analysis (BIA) it was determined that the replacement cost for each record is $30. This cost includes contacting the patient to inform them of the incident, changing the patients account numbers and printing new health cards. We can easily determine that the maximum quantitative loss associated with a full compromise of that system is $30,000. Well, that wasn't too bad, was it? Unfortunately, there is much more to consider. But does quantitative risk have to always map to money? No! When you look at the 20 controls carefully, you note that 15 of the controls can be fully automated. Internally consistent repeatable numbers can be generated that can be used to create a dashboard or report to business unit managers.

QUALITATIVE RISK ANALYSIS

Qualitative Risk Analysis focuses on a subjective analysis of risks based upon a project stakeholder's experience or judgment. Although the techniques for analyzing project risk qualitatively can be conducted by individual stakeholders, it may be more effective if done by a group. This group process allows each stakeholder to hear other points of view and supports open communication among the various stakeholders. As a result, a broader view of the threats, opportunities, issues, and points of view can be discussed and understood.

EXPECTED MONETARY VALUE

The concept of **Expected Monetary Value** provides the basis for both qualitative and quantitative risk analysis. Expected value is really an average, or mean, that takes into account both the probability and impact of various events or outcomes. For example, let's assume that a project manager of a consulting firm would like to determine the expected return or payoff associated with several possible outcomes or events. These outcomes or events, in terms of possible schedule scenarios, determine the return or profit the project will return to the consulting firm. The project manager believes each outcome has a probability of occurring and an associated payoff. The project manager's subjective beliefs are summarized in a **payoff table** below.

Expected Monetary Value of a Payoff table

Schedule Risk	A Probability	B Payoff ($)	Prob x Payoff $
Project completed 20 days early	5%	200 K	10 K
Project completed 10 days early	20%	150 K	30 K
Project completed on schedule	50%	100 K	50 K
Project completed 10 days late	20%	-	-
Project completed 20 days late	5%	(50 K)	2.5 K

As you can see from the above table, the project manager believes that the project has a small chance of finishing twenty days early or twenty days late. The payoff for finishing the project early is quite high, but there appears to be a penalty for completing the project late. As a result, the expected value or return to the consulting firm is $87,500. Since each event is mutually exclusive (i.e., only one of the five events can occur), the probabilities must sum to 100 percent.

Decision Trees

Similar to a payoff table, a decision tree provides a visual, or graphical, view of various decisions and outcomes. Let's assume that a project is going to overrun its schedule and budget. The project manager is contemplating reducing the time allocated to testing the application system as a way of bringing the project back within its original schedule and budget objectives. The project manager, then, is faced with a decision about whether the project team should conduct a full system test as planned or shorten the time originally allocated to testing.

The cost of a full test will be $10,000; but the project manager believes that there is a 95 percent chance the project will meet the quality standards set forth by the client. In this case, no additional rework will be required and no additional costs will be incurred. Since there is only a 5 percent chance the system will not meet the standards, the project manager believes that it would only require a small amount of rework to meet the quality standards. In this case, it will cost about $2,000 in resources to bring the system within standards. On the other hand, the shortened test will cost less than the full test and bring the project back on track. But, if the project team limits the testing of the system, it will very likely lower the probability of the system meeting the quality standards.

Moreover, a failure will require more rework and cost more to fix than if these problems were addressed during a full testing of the system. As you can see from above, a limited testing of the system will cost only $8,000, but the chances of the system failing to meet the quality standards increase. Moreover, the time and cost to complete the rework will be higher. Even though the project manager still has a difficult decision to make, it now becomes a more informed decision. If the project team continues with the testing activities as planned, there is a very good chance that the system will not require a great deal of rework. On the other hand, reducing the time to test the system is more of a gamble. Although there is a 30 percent chance the limited testing will save both time and money, there is a high probability that the system will not pass or meet the quality standards. As a result, the required rework will make the project even later and more over its budget. If you were the project manager, what decision would you make?

RISK IMPACT TABLE

We can create a risk impact table to analyze and prioritize various project risks. Let's use another example. Suppose a project manager has identified seven risks that could impact a particular project.

The left-hand column of risk impact table below lists the possible risks that were identified using the project risk framework introduced in the last section. For simplicity, we will focus only on risks in terms of threats, but opportunities could be analyzed and assessed using the same technique.

The second column lists the subjective probabilities for each of the risks. In this case, the probabilities do not sum to 100 percent because the risks are not mutually exclusive. In other words, none, some, or all of the risk events could occur. A probability of zero indicates that a probability has absolutely no chance of occurring, while a probability of 100 percent indicates an absolute certainty that the event will occur.

The next column provides the potential impact associated with the risk event occurring. This also is a subjective estimate based on a score from 0 to 10, with zero being no impact and ten having a very high or significant impact on the project.

Once a probability and an impact are assigned to each risk event, they are multiplied together to come up with a risk score. Although this score is based on the subjective opinions of the project stakeholders, it does provide mechanism for determining which risks should be monitored and which risks may require a response.

RISK	0 – 100% Probability	0 – 10 Impact	(P * I) Score
Key project team member leaves project	40%	4	1.6
Client unable to confirm requirements	50%	6	3.0
Client experiences financial problems	10%	9	0.9
Response time unacceptable to users	80%	6	4.8
Technology does not integrate with existing applications	60%	7	4.2
Resources may be assigned to other projects	20%	3	0.6
Customer unable to acquire licensing agreements	5%	7	0.35

"Response time unacceptable to users" and "Technology does not integrate with existing applications" are the two most significant risks to this project. The risk scores for all of the risks include the stakeholders risk tolerances and preferences since the subjective probabilities and impacts will reflect these tolerances and preferences.

Risks should be analyzed and evaluated in terms of likelihood of occurrences and magnitude of consequences if they do occur.

LIKELIHOOD				
	Likely	Medium Risk	High Risk	Extreme Risk
	Unlikely	Low Risk	Medium Risk	High Risk
	Highly Unlikely	Insignificant Risk	Low Risk	Medium Risk
		Slightly Harmful	Harmful	Extremely Harmful

CONSEQUENCES

RISK RESPONSE

The next step of the risk management process is to determine how to deal with the various project risks. In addition to resource constraints, an appropriate strategy will be determined by the project stakeholders' perceptions of risk and their willingness to take on a particular risk. Essentially, a project risk strategy will focus on one of the following approaches:

- Accept or ignore the risk.
- Avoid the risk completely.
- Reduce the likelihood or impact of the risk (or both) if the risk occurs.
- Transfer the risk to someone else (i.e., insurance).

In addition, triggers or flags in the form of metrics should be identified to draw attention to a particular risk when it occurs. This system requires that each risk have an owner to monitor the risk and to ensure that resources are made available in order to respond to the risk appropriately. Once the risks, the risk triggers, and strategies or responses are documented, this document then becomes the risk response plan.

It is not feasible or advisable to respond to each and every threat or opportunity identified because avoiding all threats or chasing after every opportunity requires resources to be diverted away from the real project work.

Therefore, the risk response strategy to a particular risk depends on:

- **The nature of the risk itself.** Is this really a threat to or opportunity for the project? How will the project be affected? At what points during the project life cycle will the project be affected? What are the triggers that would determine if a particular risk is occurring? Why should the risk be taken?

- **The impact of the risk on the project's outcomes and objectives.** A risk has a probability and an impact on the project if it occurs. What is the likelihood of this occurring? And if this risk occurs, how will the project be affected? What can be gained? What could be lost? What are the chances of success or failure?

- **The project s constraints**. Project constraints are the scope, schedule, budget, and quality requirements. Can a response to a particular threat or opportunity be made within the available resources and constraints of the project? Will additional resources be made available if a particular risk occurs? Can certain contractual obligations be waived or modified? What will happen if the desired result is not achieved?

High Impact and High Probability risks require aggressive responses.

Probability		Impact	
		Low	High
	High	Transfer (share)	Avoid (exploit)
	Low	Accept	Mitigate (Enhance)

RISK RESPONSE STRATEGY

Risk response strategies are the approaches we can make to dealing with the risks we have identified and quantified. In the section on risk quantification, we discussed evaluating the risk in terms of its impact and probability in such a way that we would be able to rank risks in their order of importance. This is what we called severity, the combination of impact and probability. Risk response strategy is really based on risk tolerance, which has been discussed. Risk tolerance in terms of severity is the point above which a risk is not acceptable and below which the risk is acceptable.

There are many reasons for selecting one risk strategy over another, and all of these factors must be considered. Cost and schedule are the most likely reasons for a given risk to have a high severity. Other factors may affect our choice of risk strategy. For example, if a schedule risk is identified for a task in the project, and if this task has many other tasks depending on it, its severity may be calculated as being lower than is apparent, and the severity should be adjusted even though the schedule impact due to the disruption may be difficult to judge. The strategy should be appropriate for the risk it is intended for.

Several strategies are available for dealing with risks. These are acceptance, transfer, avoidance, and mitigation.

RISK RESPONSE PLANNING

- **Avoidance:** Changes the project plan to eliminate the risk or protect the project objectives from the risk impact. Some risk events that arise early in the project can be avoided by clarifying requirements, obtaining information, improving communication, acquiring expertise, etc. Other examples of avoidance include: reducing scope, adding resources, extending project time, adopting familiar approaches, avoiding unfamiliar subcontractors, etc.

- **Transference**: Shifts the consequence of a risk to a third party together with ownership of the response. Most effective in dealing with financial risk exposure. Nearly always involves payment of a risk premium to the party taking on the risk. Examples include: use of insurance, performance bonds, warranties, and guarantees. Different types of contracts may also be used to transfer risk. For example, a fixed-price contract places most of the risk on the seller of the product/services whereas a cost-plus contract place most of the risk on the buyer or customer.

- **Mitigation**: Seeks to reduce the probability and/or consequences of an adverse risk event to an acceptable threshold. Taking early action helps reduce the probability of an adverse risk occurring and/or the severity of the impact and is more effective than repairing the consequences after the risk has occurred. Must take into consideration the mitigation costs given the likely probability of the risk and its consequences. Examples of mitigation include: adopting fewer complex processes, conducting more engineering tests, choosing a more stable seller, developing prototypes, adding more skilled resources, etc.

- **Acceptance:** Project team makes a conscious decision to not change the project plan to handle the risk. Project team may not be able to identify any other suitable response strategy other than accepting the risk. Active acceptance may include developing a contingency plan to execute, should a risk occur. Passive acceptance requires no action, leaving the project team to deal with the risks as they occur. A contingency plan is applied to identified risks that arise during the project. Developing a plan in advance can greatly reduce the cost of an action should the risk occur. A fallback plan is developed if the risk has a high impact, or if the selected strategy may not be fully effective. This could include allocation of a contingency amount, development of alternative options, or changing the project scope. The most usual risk acceptance response is to establish a contingency allowance or reserve which includes amounts of time, money, or resources to account for known** risks. The allowance should be determined by the impacts, computed at an acceptable level of risk exposure, for the accepted risks.

ACCEPTANCE

Choosing to accept or ignore a particular risk is a more passive approach to risk response. The project stakeholders can either be hopeful that the risk will not occur or just not worry about it unless it does. This can make sense for risks that have a low probability of occurring or a low impact. Acceptance of a risk means that the severity of the risk is low enough that we will do nothing about the risk unless it occurs. Using the acceptance strategy means that the severity of the risk is lower than our risk tolerance level. If this were not the case, it would not make sense to accept the risk. Once the risk occurs, we will fix the problem and move on. The risk is acceptable because the severity of the risk is lower than our risk tolerance.

Accepting a risk does not mean that we will not do something about the risk when and if it occurs; it means that we will do something about it only if it occurs. Many of the project risks will fall into this category. It is the category where the many insignificant risks are put. Many of these risks cost less to fix when they occur than it would cost to investigate and plan for them.

There are two kinds of acceptance, active and passive. Acceptance is active when a risk is identified as being acceptable but we decide to make a plan for what to do when and if the risk occurs. It is much more effective to have a plan in place when these types of risk occur rather than trying to deal with the risk when there is little time and lots of hysterics. There is also another risk involved: the wrong thing can be done to solve the problem because its solution was not clearly thought out under pressure in the heat of the moment.

Acceptance is passive when nothing at all is done to plan for the risk occurrence. Many of the identified risks in the project will be passively accepted. These risks are simply too small to be of concern. The cost of developing a plan and documenting it can be higher than the cost of dealing with the risk without preparation.

An example of risk acceptance is the risk that off-the-shelf software that was purchased for the project will be defective. There is a probability of 2 percent that this will occur. That is, that the CD the software is delivered on will not work and will have to be replaced with a new CD. This causes a delay of five days to a task that has twenty-five days of free float. Passive acceptance will probably be used in dealing with this risk. It is probably not worth the effort to anticipate the problem and do something about it. It is simpler to wait and see if something is wrong with the CD and take corrective action. Of course, it would be foolish to receive the CD and not test it until it was needed. In the next article, we'll look the risk strategies of transfer, avoidance, and mitigation.

TRANSFER

A transfer strategy focuses on transferring ownership of the risk to someone else. This transfer could be in the form of purchasing insurance against a particular risk or subcontracting a portion of the project work to someone who may have more knowledge or expertise in the particular area. As a result, this strategy may result in a premium, or added cost, to managing and responding to the risk.

The transfer strategy in managing risk is to give responsibility for the risk to someone outside the project. The risk does not go away; the responsibility of the risk is simply given to someone else. This can be done a number of ways. One way is to negotiate the refusal of a project deliverable that has a high risk of causing problems and have that risk contracted to another project. The stakeholder simply agrees that the deliverable is not required as part of the project and finds another project that is willing to do it.

Risks can also be transferred to a contractor working for the project. If this is done with a firm fixed price contract, the vendor will be obligated to deliver the agreed product for a fixed price. In this situation the vendor is responsible for any risks that occur while trying to complete the contract. While this may seem like a good solution to risk management problems, the vendors were not born yesterday afternoon. The vendor's risk strategy may be to increase the selling price to compensate for the risk if it occurs. Of course, if the risk does not occur the vendor will make extra money. If you try to transfer the risk in this way, it may be that you will find that you are paying for the impact of the risk whether it happens or not.

Probably the most common method of transfer is to buy insurance. With insurance you give a relatively small amount of money to an insurance company. This amount of money, called a premium, is usually much smaller than the cost of the risk. If the risk happens, the insurance company pays to have the risk resolved. If the risk does not take place, the insurance company keeps the premium.

It is interesting to note that you can insure against only your own or your company's loss. Buying insurance on someone else's life or property, for example, is not allowed in most places unless that person or property represents a loss to you. If this were not true, there would probably be people hanging around hospitals buying policies on people who looked really sick.

AVOIDANCE

The avoidance strategy focuses on taking steps to avoid the risk altogether. In this case, an active approach is made to eliminate or prevent the possibility of the threat occurring. This strategy is used to make the risk cease to be a possibility. Avoidance is a little different from the other strategies we have discussed. In risk avoidance, we completely eliminate the possibility of the risk.

The simplest way to avoid a risk is to remove it from the project deliverables. If the sponsor of the project agrees to allow a risk-filled deliverable to be removed from the project, the risk is removed along with the deliverable. Of course, the price the sponsor is paying for the project will probably be reduced to compensate for the reduction in scope. In avoiding risk in this way, we should remember that profits are often related to the risks we take to complete projects that have risks.

Another way to avoid risks is to design around them. This strategy involves changing the design of the product so that the risk cannot occur. Suppose we have a project to design and manufacture a new kind of barbecue grill. During testing we discover that the screws that hold the bottom of the grill where the ashes collect rust and deteriorate quickly. A failure of the ash collecting bottom could result in hot charcoal being dumped onto a wooden deck and causing a fire. We decide that this is an unacceptable risk and that our strategy is to avoid the risk.

One way to avoid the risk is to not build and sell the barbecue grill at all and abandon the project. We decide that this is an unnecessarily conservative strategy. Another way is to change the material that the screws are made from. Instead of plain steel screws we decide to redesign and use stainless steel screws. The stainless-steel screws will not rust, and the potential problem will be eliminated. This completely eliminates the rusting problem of the screws and avoids the risk of a screw failure causing a fire.

MITIGATION

The term mitigate means to lessen. Therefore, a mitigation risk strategy focuses on lessening the probability and/or the impact of threat if it does occur.

When we discussed risk tolerance, we said that risks that were above the risk tolerance maximum were not acceptable risks and that something had to be done about them. Mitigation is a strategy where some work is done on unacceptable risks to reduce either their probability or their impact to a point where their severity falls below the maximum risk tolerance level.

Using the risk mitigation strategy involves taking some funds out of the contingency budget that was the expected value of the risk before mitigation. Some of these funds are put into the project's operating budget to carry out the mitigation strategy.

Since the probability or impact will be reduced, the expected value of the risk will be reduced as well, and the contingency budget should be reduced accordingly.

In the next chapter we will look at all four response strategies again in terms of what each means to allocating dollars to your projects.

Risk Tolerance

Risk tolerance is the willingness of some person or some organization to accept or avoid risk. In any group of people there are gamblers or risk takers and there are non-gamblers or risk avoiders. People who have a low willingness to accept risks and the consequences of risks are called risk avoiders. Those people who are willing to take risks are called risk takers.

It is important to know that people and organizations have differing risk tolerances. Some customers do not want to risk the delivery of the project they are paying for by taking a chance on something new. Other customers will welcome the opportunity if the danger is not too great. For example, if we were manufacturing a product like some of the products that are advertised on late-night television, we would probably have a relatively high-risk tolerance for the product's failure. This is because the product is priced very low and is not going to put anyone's life in danger. Customers buying very low-priced items can expect them to have a shorter useful life than the advertising indicates. If customers want a product that will last longer, they buy an item that is built better and is probably more expensive.

This ability to choose is related to risk tolerance. In the mind of the consumer there is a tolerance for risk, which is expressed in his or her willingness to spend money. A consumer who is interested in having a highly reliable product that will last a long time is willing to pay more to get these features. Another consumer who is not willing to pay more to get a better product will be more accepting of the risk that the product will fail.

Risk tolerance is somewhat describable in monetary terms. Our risk tolerance is how much we are willing to lose if the risk happens. In the case of a product that is sold to a consumer, the cost of the failure of the product might be the cost of the repair or replacement of the product if it fails. In the situation where someone's life is in danger, these decisions become much more important. The tolerance for a risk that is life-threatening is very high indeed. This is because we cannot put a monetary value on human life.

RISK MONITORING AND CONTROL

Once the salient project risks have been identified and appropriate responses formulated, the next step entails scanning the project environment so that both identified and unidentified threats and opportunities can be followed, much like a radar screen follows ships. Risk owners should monitor the various risk triggers so that well-informed decisions and appropriate actions can take place.

In this final chapter, we shall look at what risk monitoring and control is and how we monitor and track the risks that are identified and new ones that are encountered on our projects. Once the risk response plan is created, the various risk triggers must be continually monitored to keep track of the various project risks. In addition, new threats and opportunities may present themselves over the course of the project, so it is important that the project stakeholders be vigilant.

Risk monitoring and control is part of the project monitoring and control of the project management life cycle. Monitoring and control focus on metrics to help identify when a risk occurs, and also on communication. This chapter addresses how important it is to have a good monitoring and control system that supports communication among the various stakeholders and provides information essential to making timely and effective decisions.

The process of monitoring and controlling and keeping track of the identified and the unidentified risks is risk control. In this process we hope to identify risks that are no longer possible and risks that are coming due, as well as any new risks that may become evident. We will also monitor risk activity to make sure the risk plans have been carried out successfully. Problems that have been found out in the risk plan can help us adjust the plans for future risk activities.

Risk control and monitoring are part of the risk management process and must be started early in the project and continued until the end. As the project progresses, we will find that many of the risks will change, some will no longer be possible, others will happen and be disposed of, and new risks will be identified. In addition, we will learn about the project and the risks associated with it and adjust our vision of individual risks. The level of risk tolerance should be monitored as well. The attitude of the stakeholders will change during the course of the project. Communication with all stakeholders is important since it gives us a means of assessing changes in their risk tolerance.

Risk control may involve changing the way we look at risk. There are several reasons why this might take place. The risk tolerance of the stakeholders may change; the risk tolerance of the project team may change. As the project progresses toward its completion, certain risks that were thought to be very important to the success of the project may become risks that are no longer thought of as being so important.

Chapter 10 : SAFETY AND COMPLIANCE

An engineering manager ensures that the organization conducts its business processes in compliance with laws and regulations, professional standards, international standards, and accepted business practices. Engineering manager perform audits at regular intervals and execute design control systems, advising the management on possible risks that might occur, and organization policies. The major task of an engineering manager is to uphold the ethical integrity of the organization and also ensure that business activities are conducted using a regulatory framework. These professionals carry out the risk management process by thorough planning of business and implementing the policies within the organization.

Engineering managers are considered to be a vital component of corporate governance. They are also responsible to determine how an organization should be handled and governed. These responsibilities include maintaining good rapport between the stakeholders and adhering to the objectives set by the organization.

The roles and responsibilities of an engineering manager vary depending upon the industry, but typical responsibilities are described below:

- They are accountable for ensuring all the essential guidelines are put in proper place accurately adhering to industry rules and regulations.
- They conduct internal audits and reviews at regular intervals to ensure that compliance procedures are regularly followed.
- They conduct environmental audits adhering to environmental standards.
- The engineering manager role involves the safety of employees and businesses as well. It's their part of duty to ensure all the tasks are done with higher accuracy.

- They have to ensure that all the employees are thoroughly updated about the organization's policies, regulations, and processes
- They should advise the management regarding the implementation of compliance programs associated with asset maintenance.
- They must adhere to the training and supervising the staff that needs attention to rules and regulations.

Fire Risk Assessment

It is important to carry out a fire risk assessment appropriate to the particular workplace. It is also good practice to involve staff in the process, as they may have identified a potential fire risk of which people higher up the organization may not be aware.

The two most important questions to ask are:

- How likely is it for a fire to start in my workplace?
- How easy is it for employees, and other people who may be affected, to escape to a place of safety in the event of a fire?

In larger workplaces, it is good policy to carry out a separate inspection for each significantly different section, area or department. The whole of the work place should be taken into account, including any outdoor areas and any rooms or parts of buildings that are not currently in use. Even if the workplace has been subject to previous approvals by the various enforcing authorities for other safety, licensing or building legislation, you are still required to carry out an assessment of your fire precautions. However, if there has been no significant change in the workplace, for example, in the number of employees or the activities which they undertake, it is unlikely that any significant additional fire precautions will have to be provided. If you do propose to make changes to your fire precautions as a result of carrying out a fire risk assessment, these must not conflict with the controls imposed by other legislation. If in any doubt, you are advised to consult a fire safety officer from your local fire service.

If other employers share your premises, your organization has a responsibility to ensure that they are made aware of any significant risks and any action you have taken to reduce that risk. In addition, you should take all reasonable steps to coordinate your fire safety measures with those of any other employers who may share your workplace.

IDENTIFY FIRE HAZARDS

Potential fire hazards in the workplace will include potential sources of ignition, sources of fuel and any hazards associated with the processes carried out in the workplace. Identify the location of people at significant risk in case of fire This step needs to take into account not only employees, but other people who may be in the premises, such as customers, members of the public, visitors and contractors. The special needs of any disabled staff and visitors must also be considered. There may be parts of the premises where people are more at risk than others.

EVALUATE THE RISKS

This step involves deciding whether existing fire precautions are adequate, or whether improvements are required to remove the hazard or to control the risk. It is necessary to look at any existing fire safety measures provided in terms of:

- the control of ignition and fuel sources
- fire detection and fire warning systems
- means of escape
- means of fighting fire
- maintenance and testing of fire precautions

- fire safety training for employees.

The nature of the risk evaluation will depend very much on the nature of the workplace and the work activities carried out.

RECORD FINDINGS AND ACTION TAKEN

The engineering manager requires organizations that employ five or more people to record the significant findings of the assessment and any group of employees identified as being especially at risk. There is a legal requirement to provide employees with 'comprehensive and relevant information'. This means telling employees or their representatives about the risk assessment findings, and perhaps making the formal risk assessment report available to them on request.

KEEP ASSESSMENT UNDER REVIEW

It is good practice to carry out an annual review of the workplace to ensure that no new risks have developed as a result of, for example, changes to work processes, machinery, substances or the number of people likely to be present in the workplace. There should also be a reassessment of the workplace if you have carried out alterations or extensions, as they may have affected the fire precautions previously provided.

FIRE RISK ASSESSMENT CHECKLIST

Escape routes

- Are main and emergency stairways protected by self-closing fire doors?
- Is the emergency route clearly sign posted?
- Are there any 'dead end' conditions where escape is possible in one direction only?

- Is all escape routes clear of obstruction?
- Are all exit doors unobstructed externally?
- Are there enough exits?
- Are exit doors free to open at all times (not locked)?
- Are fire doors fitted with 'fire door keep shut' signs, and is this instruction followed?

Fire Defense Equipment

- Is the fire alarm system satisfactory for the risk?
- Will it meet current legal requirements?
- Is the fire alarm, hydrants, fire extinguishers/hose reels, sprinklers and emergency lighting maintained by qualified people? Is maintenance recorded in a logbook?
- Is the fire alarm tested weekly?
- Does the fire alarm have automatic fire detectors in corridors, stairways and risk rooms?
- Are routine checks made to ensure that equipment has not been obscured, moved or damaged?

Work Equipment and *Furnishings*

- Are all items of portable electrical equipment inspected regularly and fitted with correctly rated fuses?
- Is the wiring of electrical installations inspected periodically by a competent electrical engineer?
- Are the use of extension leads and multipoint adapters kept to a minimum?
- Are flexible electrical leads run in safe places where they will not be easily damaged?

- Is upholstery in good condition?

Cleanliness and Tidiness

- Are staff encouraged to tidy their personal workplaces?
- Are the premises kept clear of combustible waste?
- Are metal bins with closely fitting lids available for waste such as floor sweepings?
- Are separate, clearly labeled containers provided for waste and special hazards, such as flammable liquids, paint rags, and oily rags?
- Are waste containers removed from the building at the end of each working day or more frequently if necessary?
- Is waste disposal put in a safe place which is not accessible to the public?
- Is the burning of waste on site prohibited?
- Are cupboards, lift shafts, spaces under benches, gratings, conveyor belts and similar places kept free from dust and the accumulation of rubbish?
- Are pipes, beams, trusses, ledges, ducting and electrical fittings regularly cleaned?
- Are areas in and around the building kept free from accumulated packaging materials and pallets?
- Are metal lockers provided for employees' clothing?

Storage

- Are fire doors, exits, fire equipment and fire notices kept unobstructed?
- Are storage areas accessible to firefighters?
- Are stack sizes kept as small as possible?

- Are there adequate gangways between stacks?
- Are stacks stable?
- Are stocks of material arranged so that sprinkler heads and fire detectors are not impeded and are the required clearances beneath this equipment maintained?
- Are excessive quantities of stock avoided?
- Is access to storage areas restricted to those who need to be there?
- Is stock kept well clear of light fixtures and hot service pipes?

MAINTENANCE OF BUILDINGS

- Is every point of entry to the site and building secure against intruders?
- After the closedown of operations are all doors, windows, and gates checked and secure?
- Is the building regularly inspected for damage to windows, roof and walls?
- Are the grounds surrounding the premises kept free of combustible vegetation by regular grass cutting and scrub clearance?
- Are all outside contractors supervised while on the premises and their work authorized by 'permit to work' schemes?

HEATING AND LIGHTING

- Are there restrictions on using unauthorized heaters?

- Are combustible materials at a safe distance from appliances and flues?
- Is care taken that no materials are left on heaters?
- Are portable heaters securely guarded and placed where they cannot be knocked over or ignite combustibles?
- Are goods kept clear of lighting equipment?

SMOKING

- Is smoking prohibited in all but designated external 'smoking' areas?
- Where smoking is permitted are there enough ashtrays or other disposal facilities?

STAFF TRAINING

- Are new staff instructed in fire procedures and shown the fire escape routes on their first day at work?
- Are fire action notices posted throughout the workplace?
- Are there trained fire marshals?
- Is there a designated fire assembly point?
- Have staff had the opportunity to operate a fire extinguisher?
- Do staff know how to deal with the disabled, the public and visitors in the event of an evacuation?

COMPLIANCE IN ASSOCIATION WITH FACILITIES MANAGEMENT

In recent years, throughout the world we have followed the high level of corruption in various economic sectors. Several companies end up having their image and reputation weakened due to their proven involvement, both at the business level and in the political sphere. The imperative need to know and practice compliance in day-to-day activities arose in the midst of this reality, which affects companies of all sizes and industries. The concept of compliance in relation to facilities management aims to generate value for an organization and ensure its survival.

This practice arises from the great financial impacts caused by factors such as:

- Absence of normative guidelines
- Misalignments to applicable laws
- Lack of adequate preventative tools
- Process management failures
- Operations without a structured information system.

The verb comply means to conform to a rule, which explains much of the concept of the word. The meaning of the word compliance is related to the conduct of a company and its compliance with the rules of regulatory bodies. What is compliance in business, in short? It means to comply with laws and regulations. This concept covers all the policies, rules, internal and external controls to which an organization must conform. When in compliance, an organization's activities will be in full accordance with the rules and laws applied to its processes. Both the company and all its people, including suppliers of interest, need to behave in accordance with the rules of regulatory bodies. In addition, they must ensure faithful compliance with the various internal normative instruments. Only in this way will the company comply with regulations for environment, labor, finance, work safety, operations, accounting, etc.

HOW IMPORTANT IS COMPLIANCE IN FACILITIES MANAGEMENT?

Being able to say that a company is in strategic compliance is by itself a fundamental business strategy. It means that there is transparency and an increasing degree of management maturity. Being in compliance shows that facility managers and teams are in control of the processes and procedures, implemented and executed with effective political, commercial, labor, contractual and regulatory compliance. Not being in compliance means being unnecessarily high risk, which can lead to financial, equity and market losses, among many others. Risk management and compliance are closely linked. It is necessary to reflect and change management styles, adjust the way company information is handled and how people behave on a day-to-day basis, in order to achieve a level of excellence in compliance regardless of the business sector and size of the company.

How To Align Facilities Management with The Concept of Compliance

Now that you know what compliance in business is, check out some tips:

- Use information systems that support monitoring of the company's activities and that conform to compliance processes.
- Have contract management for services and materials that is aligned with the levels of compliance established by the company.
- Strengthen inspection and inspection routines of activities, including those that do not usually have certifications.
- Focus on process compliance at the municipal, state, and federal levels.
- Have an active and updated system of standardization in the company.
- Have internal audit processes focused on the requirements to achieve compliance.
- Have control systems with adequate depth degrees.
- Have structured communication about the normative instruments of the company.

What is a Compliance Framework?

Formally, a compliance framework is a structured set of guidelines to aggregate, harmonize, and integrate all the compliance requirements that apply to your organization. In practice, a compliance framework lets you take a collection of documents, policy manuals, procedure descriptions, mission statements, regulatory mandates, control documentation and meld those things into one cohesive whole. A compliance framework brings order to the ceaseless stream of regulatory mandates that rain down on a large organization so that when something new comes along, you have a method for integrating that new requirement into your existing approach to compliance. Compliance frameworks are usually tailored to a specific issue. For example, you might follow one framework to guide your anti-graft compliance, another to guide your data privacy compliance, and a third to guide anti-discrimination compliance. Your compliance program would use those frameworks to measure its progress on all three issues.

WHY DO COMPLIANCE FRAMEWORKS EXIST?

Compliance frameworks exist to help compliance officers build a compliance program efficiently. You would miss too many steps, or take certain steps out of ideal order and end up repeating your work, or repeat the same step over and over and waste program resources. Some parts of the enterprise might be managing compliance risk brilliantly, while another part is managing the same risk terribly and you, the compliance officer, might not be aware of the discrepancy. Which could lead to awkward conversations with regulators if you experience a compliance failure, and those regulators start asking about the effectiveness of your compliance program.

Let's remember that all large organizations already have at least some compliance activities happening around their enterprise, and many will even have quite a lot of compliance activity happening. Your job as a compliance officer is to wrestle all that activity into one disciplined program that meets all the regulatory obligations your company has. A compliance framework lets you proceed through that work in a methodical way, so you can reap the most benefit for the least expense of time, resources and your own sanity!

Moreover, compliance frameworks provide a standard that others can use to judge your compliance program. That is, when regulators or the board, or auditors, or business partners ask, "How strong is your compliance program? You can map your program and its activities to what those frameworks require. Those parties can then better understand the program improvements you have already made or the ones you still need to make.

COMPLIANCE WITH COMPANY POLICIES

A policy is a written statement about how your company views certain risks. It can be a simple rule that states what the company's compliance objective is. For example, for anti-bribery, the policy could be something like the one below:

The company is committed to conducting its business in an ethical, honest, and transparent manner. Bribery and corruption are not consistent with our values, and present significant risks to its business. Therefore, employees should never offer, give, solicit, or accept a bribe; whether cash or other inducement to or from any person or company. The company is committed to the prevention, deterrence, and detection of bribery and corruption.

Corporate policies are the backbone of a compliance program. Unto itself, however, a policy usually does little to teach employees or agents and other third parties how to act when faced with a particular temptation or risk. That's where procedures come in.

WHAT ARE COMPLIANCE PROCEDURES?

Procedures provide employees and agents with guidance about how to act under certain circumstances, to ensure that they don't violate corporate policies.

For example, you could require employees to seek approval from the legal or finance department demonstrating a legitimate business purpose before offering to pay travel and lodging expenses for a foreign government official. You could also require prospective agents to complete a due diligence questionnaire, or have employees complete their own due diligence checklists as part of the agent pre-hire process.

A compliance framework will help you understand what procedures you should put into place. A framework can identify which ones make the most sense for your organization, and clarify the work that will be necessary to put those procedures into effect.

What Are Compliance Controls?

Controls, by contrast, are specific checks or gateways intended to prevent improper transactions from happening. They are usually administered by accounting or compliance personnel or, even better, are automated parts of your IT systems to help assure that policies and procedures are not subverted. For example, a control could be something as simple as requiring two authorized signatures on an approval to spend money entertaining a foreign official; or as complex as disallowing any payment to an agent or reseller whose due diligence is not already complete. Another might be to disallow any spending requests at all from employees who have not completed necessary anti-bribery training or policy attestations. All controls aim at the same goal, that is to control and oversight of corporate transactions, so those transactions unfold according to company policy and regulatory obligations.

Spotting hazards

Ways of identifying hazards include asking employees or their safety representatives what risks they have noticed; consulting accident and ill-health records, suppliers 'manuals, the trade press, relevant legislation and guidance; or seeking advice from consultants.

Typical hazards to watch for include:
- physical hazards (e.g., poorly guarded machinery, mezzanine floors, slipping/ tripping hazards, vehicles, poor electrical wiring, fire hazards)

- hazardous substances (e.g., chemicals, dust, fumes)
- a hazardous work environment (e.g., noise, poor ventilation, bad lighting, hot or cold workplaces)
- psychological hazards (e.g., stress, long hours, shift work)
- ergonomic hazards (e.g., repetitive work, lifting).

WHO MAY BE HARMED?

Those at risk may be:

- employees (e.g., office, operational and maintenance staff)
- contractors (e.g., cleaners and security guards)
- members of the public and volunteers
- young and inexperienced workers
- new and expectant mothers
- staff with disabilities
- home, lone and mobile workers.

Risks may increase at certain times of day, such as after dark or during busy periods.

CONTROLLING THE RISKS

It is important to consider whether existing precautions:

- meet legal requirements
- comply with industry standards
- represent good practice
- reduce risks as far as reasonably practicable.

If not, an action plan will be necessary, categorizing remaining risks as high, medium or low risk. Priority should go to those measures that will protect the whole workplace. The aim is to eliminate hazards altogether (e.g., by not using a hazardous substance) or, if this is not possible, to control risks, in order of preference, by:

- combating risks at source (e.g., if steps are slippery, treating them is better than displaying a warning sign)
- preventing access to the hazard (e.g., by installing machine guards, using permits to work which restrict access to authorized staff, isolating a dusty area)
- organizing work to reduce exposure to the hazard (e.g., by rearranging work patterns to reduce stress)
- issuing Personal Protection Equipment (PPE)
- providing welfare facilities (e.g., washing facilities to remove contamination).

Taking advantage of technical advances can make work processes safer and more efficient. It is also crucial to provide relevant training and information to staff, and in shared workplaces, to swap information with other firms on site.

RECORDING THE FINDINGS

Generally speaking, organizations with five or more employees must write down their risk assessment. The document can make cross-references to the health and safety policy and other relevant paperwork, rather than repeating everything. An inspector or a union safety representative may ask to see the risk assessment, or it may provide evidence in the event of a personal injury claim.

REVIEWING AND REVISING

Most health and safety legislation require employers to review the risk assessment and revise it as necessary, if it is 'no longer valid or there has been a significant change'. Hazardous substance and asbestos assessments must, however, be reviewed 'regularly', and HSE guidance states that this is good practice for any risk assessment. Significant changes that may make the risk assessment out of date could include bringing in new machines, substances or procedures.

The Management Regulations require risk assessments to be 'suitable and sufficient'. This means:

- allocating appropriate resources
- making the level of detail proportionate to the risk: overcomplicated assessments of simple hazards are not required
- anticipating 'foreseeable' risks
- ensuring that consultants have sufficient understanding of particular work activities
- adapting any 'model' assessment to the actual work situation
- drawing up a timetable for implementing short, medium and long-term controls
- reviewing non-routine activities such as maintenance, cleaning, loading and unloading vehicles, changes in production cycles and emergencies
- reviewing off-site activities, such as home working
- complying with specific regulations; although repeating assessments is not necessary
- addressing what actually happens in the workplace, not what the works manual says should happen.

Chapter 11 : TIME MANAGEMENT

WHAT IS TIME MANAGEMENT SKILLS?

Time is the most valuable of all because once lost it never comes back! If you want to achieve something worthwhile in life you must as well start mastering Time management skills. It is the skill set that enables you to become more efficient and have more time to do the things that's useful for you rather than getting stuck in things that will take you nowhere!

An efficient manager, a happy spouse and a good parent all have one thing in common. They have mastered the art of time management skills. Among all the soft skills the most important is undoubtedly Time management skills. At the end of the day if you want to improve your personal and professional lives you must start learning this skill from now on.

BENEFITS OF HAVING GOOD TIME MANAGEMENT SKILLS

To think of it the benefits of Time management skills are plenty, some of the important ones are given below.

1. You get more time to do things you love

So, what do you do when you manage time more effectively? You get free time that you can use it as per your wish. Learn a language, or attend an event, visit your mother or call your brother, you get to choose whatever you want to do in the available time. Simply put, you have more opportunities to spend time on things and people that matter to you even after your daily work schedule!

2. You reach your goals

With an effective time, management strategy, you stay focused on your goals and reach them easily. Because when you use your time wisely you do not waste it! So, instead of watching the new Web series, you end up listening to a podcast that gives you direction to your goal. Or you hone a skill or read a book that ultimately leads you to your cherished ambition. Therefore, you are conscious that time is not wasted but utilized appropriately!

3. You stay updated

A huge advantage of managing time effectively is that you stay on track of everything. You know what's happening, what's expected from you, and as a result, you plan your day accordingly.

4. You would be praised by everyone

A good time manager is praised by everyone. It's not sufficient to mention it in your cover letter, you must as well prove it in your workplace! If you know how to manage your time you become more productive. You will be noticed and admired at your workplace for your quality of delivering projects on time. On the personal front, your family will appreciate you when you give them the time they deserve. You will get time to have a social life too and your friends and relatives would be impressed when you spend good amounts of time with them.

5. *You lead a stress-free life*

When you rush on a regular basis unable to meet the deadlines and always lack focus and control, you become stressed. Your work efficiency gets reduced and you get a bad reputation at the office. But when you improve your time management skills you start completing all your tasks on time. You get a lot of free time for relaxation and fun. Being an effective time manager, your life becomes organized and stress levels are lowered.

THE VALUE OF TIME

You may have seen this popular, uncredited e-mail that has widely circulated on the Internet:

- To realize the value of one year, ask a student who failed a grade.
- To realize the value of one month, ask a mother who gave birth to a premature baby.

- To realize the value of one week, ask the editor of a weekly newspaper.
- To realize the value of one hour, ask the lovers who are waiting to meet.
- To realize the value of one second, ask the person who just avoided a traffic accident.
- To realize the value of one millisecond, ask the person who won an Olympic medal.
- Time has a value greater than any currency. We may leave our children the money we don't use in our own lifetimes, but we cannot leave them one millisecond of time.

Before you can decide what kinds of changes you want to make both in your professional career and in your personal life you need to understand what kinds of choices (many of them subconscious) you're already making. You need to ask yourself some hard questions, delve deeply, and be brutally honest with yourself in answering them. In short, you need a picture of both your natural organizational style and the ways in which that style both supports and undermines your relationship with time.

THE FIRST STEP

Start by taking a "snapshot" of your time management style. It will be a good first step on the way to understanding your behavior patterns. Check each item you answer "yes" to:

- Do you have a daily calendar (print or electronic) that you carry with you to and from work?
- Do you make a copy of every document you sign?
- Do you have maps in your car? If you don't have a car, would you keep maps in your car if you had one?

- Do you usually reconfirm appointments that were made some time ago?
- Do you try to return a phone call within 24 hours?
- In your home right now, do you have a customary place for your keys?
- Do you keep most of your service manuals (e.g., for home appliances, computers, TVs) in a place where you can find them quickly?
- At home right now, are there a pad and a pencil next to the phone?
- Is there an official, set time when someone looking for you will find you in your office?
- If you were to get sick tomorrow, would there be someone who could step in and handle your responsibilities at work with reasonable efficiency?
- Do you have a filing system at home for your personal papers?
- If the light bulb in the main lighting fixture in your living room were to burn out tonight, would you have another bulb at home in storage to replace it?
- Do you ever take with you a material to read when waiting to see a doctor?

If you found that eight or more of the above statements could apply to you, you almost certainly have solid management skills. If you identified with 11 or more, that's great unless your well-organized behavior is obsessive. If you found fewer than eight statements applied, you probably have some work to do.

THE SECOND STEP

Now take a close look at the following questions. Check those you would answer in the affirmative.

- Have you had an unintentional finance charge in the last three months?
- Do you take work home more than once a week?
- Do you stay at work beyond your official working hours more than twice a week?
- While in school, did you frequently cram before a test?
- Are you presently on a committee that bores you?
- Do you often put off returning a call to someone you don't like, even if it's important?
- Do you wait until you have a dental problem to see your dentist?
- Do you frequently skip breakfast?
- Do slips of paper with phone numbers, addresses, etc., tend to pile up in your purse or wallet, on your desk, in your pockets, etc.?

These questions assess whether certain deep-seated habits or environmental factors undermine the efficiency of your lifestyle. You might want to reread each question to get a few clues as to where you might need some work. If you have five or more yes answers, you need to consider some serious behavioral or environmental reprogramming. And unless you have a score of 0, there are facets of your life that need improvement.

TAKING CONTROL

Make a list of items and activities that you confront on a daily or near-daily basis. Assign each a numerical value from 1 to 5, with 1 representing an item over which you have no control and 5 an item over which you have complete control. For example, you have complete control over how you respond to the ringing of your alarm clock in the morning. You also have at least some controls over whether or not you answer the telephone when it rings more control, perhaps, at home than in the office. You may have absolutely no control of morning traffic, but you do have control over your reaction to it. Begin by attempting to take more control of items you currently value as 4's that is, not quite complete control, but almost. As you master these, begin with the 3's. And once a month, for the next six months, update your list and your valuations, reevaluating the level of control you're actually able to exert over each item. As you become more conscious of both the need to take control and your power to exercise control, you should begin to see a steady improvement in your "control ratings".

WHERE DO THE HOURS GO?

How many hours do you spend a week watching TV? During which hour do you receive the most phone calls at work? How much reading do you do weekly? Think out your answers before reading ahead. If you're an average American, each week you watch TV for 25 hours, read for just under three hours, and receive the most phone calls between 10 and 11 a.m. Do these figures match your time utilization? If not, is it because you are not typical, or because you under- or overestimated? Most people have a poorly defined sense of how they spend their time. Even if you have a good sense of how you allocate your time, an inventory of how much time you spend doing various activities may reveal a surprise or two. A very useful diagnostic exercise would be to carry a small notebook with you for a few days and jot down your activities, indicating the time it took you to do each thing. You might want to do this just for your business activities but you'll find the experiment even more revealing if you include your personal time as well. An analysis of your time allocation experiment results should include:

- The two most time-consuming activities in your daily work life.
- The two most time-consuming activities in your personal life.
- The two activities most surprising to you in how much time they consume.
- The two activities most surprising to you in how little time they consume.
- An honest appraisal of which activities you feel should consume less of your time.
- An honest appraisal of which activities you feel should consume more of your time.

The conclusions you draw from this exercise, and from an honest assessment of your time management style, should aid you in identifying those areas of your professional and personal life that could most benefit from change. You may find you need a renewed or decreased emphasis on various factors that affect your time management approach. Or, perhaps, applying more thoughtful time management techniques would be useful to you. You might even decide you need a more comprehensive practice of organizational strategies throughout all phases of your life.

THE ABC SYSTEM

Preached by virtually every time management expert and practiced by more organization-sensitive people than any other method, the ABC system is the "grandfather" of prioritizing strategies. In a nutshell, it says that all tasks can and should be given an A, B, C value:

- Tasks are those that must be done, and soon. When accomplished, A tasks may yield extraordinary results. Left undone, they may generate serious, unpleasant, or disastrous consequences. Immediacy is what an A priority is all about.

- B tasks are those that should be done soon. Not as pressing as A tasks, they're still important. They can be postponed, but not for too long. Within a brief time, though, they can easily rise to A status.

- C tasks are those that can be put off without creating dire consequences. Some can linger in this category almost indefinitely. Others especially those tied to a distant completion date will eventually rise to A or B levels as the deadline approaches.

- D tasks are those that, theoretically, don't even need to be done. They're rarely anchored to deadlines. They would be nice to accomplish but realistically could be totally ignored, with no obvious adverse or severe effects. Strangely, though, when you attend to them (often when you have nothing better to do), they can yield surprising benefits. A few examples: reading an old magazine that turns out to contain a valuable article, buying a new reading lamp for your desk that improves your work environment dramatically, browsing through a stationery store and discovering an organizational tool that will make your filing much easier, or rereading your cell phone instructions to find out some wonderful functions you never knew it had.

Applying this system to your own situation should help to give you a clearer sense of how it works. Make a list, for example, of 10 things you would ideally like to accomplish tomorrow. Then select from this list four items that you really expect to do, ranking them in order of importance. The first two will be A tasks and the second two B tasks. Now, from your list of 10 choose two more items that will probably be on your mind tomorrow but can be put off, if necessary. These are C tasks. The remaining four items are most likely D tasks: nice to do but in no way pressing. You might do them tomorrow if you have nothing better to do and feel ambitious or motivated.

Prioritizing Your Tasks

How do you decide the relative importance of various tasks? Below are five criteria by which you can weigh tasks when assigning them priorities:

1. High payoffs. Which tasks will provide the best return on investment for your time and energy?
2. Essential to your goals. Which tasks are absolutely critical for meeting personal and professional goals?
3. Essential to your company's goals. Which tasks will most benefit your company, providing it with the best return on investment for employing you?
4. Essential to your boss's goals. Which tasks does your boss regard as most important?
5. Can't be delegated. Which tasks can be done only by you? These will be high priorities.

The best time to set priorities is the afternoon or evening before not the morning. That way, you can sleep on your priority list and then review it in the morning. You may spot some things you want to change.

THE ABCS OF PRIORITIZING

These approaches can facilitate your prioritizing:

- Label every task you list in your organizer with a letter value. An assumption: you have some sort of organizer, either electronic or paper. Just doing this may prompt you to rearrange the time order of some of the things you have "penciled in."

- Fill out a to-do list in random order, then label each item with a rating. This list should drive your scheduling.

- Equip your desk with a three- or four-tray filing system. Label the top tray the A tray, the next down the B tray, and so forth. Place each project, etc., in a folder and file it in the appropriate tray. Every morning, review the A's and B's, moving items up as needed. Check through the C's and D's every Friday morning to detect tasks that you need to move up.

This important distinction, when assigning priorities, is a matter of time. A task is urgent when it must be done immediately. Such a task may be less important, in the long run, than other, more critical (that is, extremely important) tasks, but its importance is magnified by the fact that it's extremely time-sensitive. So, it's always critical to schedule urgent tasks first, even if the importance of the task (all other things being equal) would make it a B rather than an A.

Chapter 12 :   PROBLEM-SOLVING

When employers talk about problem-solving skills, they are often referring to the ability to handle difficult or unexpected situations in the workplace as well as complex business challenges. Organizations rely on people who can assess both kinds of situations and calmly identify solutions. Problem-solving skills are traits that enable you to do that. While problem-solving skills are valued by employers, they are also highly useful in other areas of life like relationship building and day-to-day decision-making.

Problem-solving skills help you determine the source of a problem and find an effective solution. Although problem-solving is often identified as its own separate skill, there are other related skills that contribute to this ability.

Some key problem-solving skills include:
- Active listening
- Analysis
- Research
- Creativity
- Communication
- Decision-making
- Team-building

Problem-solving skills are important in every career at every level. As a result, effective problem solving may also require industry or job-specific technical skills. For example, a registered nurse will need active listening and communication skills when interacting with patients but will also need effective technical knowledge related to diseases and medications. In many cases, a nurse will need to know when to consult a doctor regarding a patient's medical needs as part of the solution.

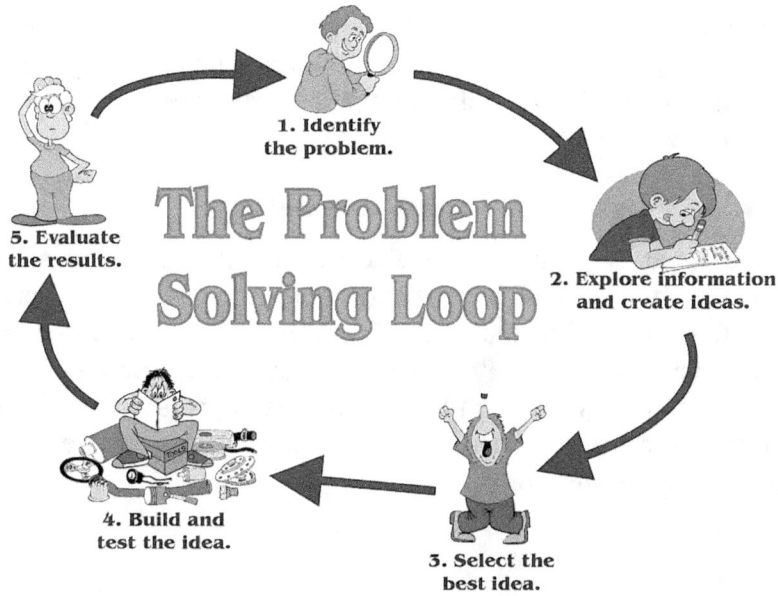

PROBLEM-SOLVING SKILLS EXAMPLES

To solve a problem effectively, you will likely use a few different skills. Here are a few examples of skills you may use when solving a problem:

Research

Researching is an essential skill related to problem solving. As a problem solver, you need to be able to identify the cause of the issue and understand it fully. You can begin to gather more information about a problem by brainstorming with other team members, consulting more experienced colleagues or acquiring knowledge through online research or courses.

Analysis

The first step to solving any problem to analyze the situation. Your analytical skills will help you understand problems and effectively develop solutions. You will also need analytical skills during research to help distinguish between effective and ineffective solutions.

Decision-making

Ultimately, you will need to make a decision about how to solve problems that arise. At times and with industry experience) you may be able to make a decision quickly. Solid research and analytical skills can help those who have less experience in their field. There may also be times when it is appropriate to take some time to craft a solution or escalate the issue to someone more capable of solving it.

Communication

When identifying possible solutions, you will need to know how to communicate the problem to others. You will also need to know what communication channels are the most appropriate when seeking assistance. Once you find a solution, communicating it clearly will help reduce any confusion and make implementing a solution easier.

Dependability

Dependability is one of the most important skills for problem-solvers. Solving problems in a timely manner is essential. Employers highly value individuals they can trust to both identify and then implement solutions as fast and effectively as possible.

How To Improve Your Problem-Solving Skills

There are several methods you can use to improve your problem-solving skills. Whether you are searching for a job or currently working, improving your problem-solving skills and associated abilities will help make you a strong candidate and employee.

Acquire More Technical Knowledge in Your Field

Depending on your industry, it may be easier to solve problems if you have strong working technical knowledge. You can more technical knowledge through additional coursework, training or practice.

Seek Out Opportunities to Problem Solve

By putting yourself into new situations, you are more likely to be exposed to opportunities to problem solve. You may find there are opportunities to volunteer for new projects in your current role, on another team or outside the workplace for another organization.

Do Practice Problems

Practice and role-play can be useful tools when learning to develop your problem-solving skills. You can find professional practice books for your industry and problem-solving scenarios online. Practice how you might solve those problems and determine if your potential solutions are viable.

For example, in customer service you might find a scenario like, "How would you handle an angry customer?" or "How do you respond when a customer asks for a refund?" Practicing how you might handle these or other scenarios common in your industry can help you call upon solutions quickly when they arise on the job.

Observe How Others Problem Solve

You may have colleagues who are skilled problem solvers. Observing how those colleagues solve problems can help you improve your own skills. If possible, ask one of your more experienced colleagues if you can observe their techniques. Asking relevant questions can be helpful in applying them in your own career.

PROBLEM-SOLVING ACTIVITIES FOR TEAM BUILDING

If you work on a team or you lead a team, it can be helpful to host occasional team-building activities to sharpen your team's problem-solving skills while having fun. In this article, we explain three problem-solving activities that can help you build a stronger team.

BENEFITS OF PROBLEM-SOLVING ACTIVITIES IN TEAM BUILDING

Problem-solving activities in team building are an effective way to improve teamwork and collaboration. This is because teams are designed to resolve problems. Essentially, you are allowing your employees to practice being a team without any of the normal stressors of the workplace. One benefit of problem-solving activities in team building is the ability to present employees with challenges they normally would not encounter. This lets you test the team in new ways, which forces team members to think with unconventional methods. In many cases, this leads to employees changing how they work to find new solutions. Teams bring these changes back to the workplace where they can help solve existing problems.

PROBLEM-SOLVING TEAM-BUILDING ACTIVITIES

Problem-solving team-building activities are an effective way to improve team collaboration. The key to making them effective is having well-planned activities. These activities must facilitate shared experiences that bring team members closer together. Here are several problem-solving team-building activities to try.

The collapsing space game

There are many variations of the collapsing space game used in problem-solving team building, but the purpose remains the same. The game is designed to improve a team's ability to adapt to changing situations while incorporating input from every individual.

This game is simple to play and only requires something to mark the boundary of the team's workspace. The key is to limit the team's space in a way that is easy to change and can fit the entire team. A rope is usually the best choice, but your team can also play the game with other physical boundary markers. To play, place the team inside the boundary made with the rope or other markers. The team must stay inside the boundary at all times. Over time, reduce the size of the team's space by shrinking the boundary. The team will have to adapt to find new ways of keeping everyone inside the boundary.

The Emergency plan game

Another easy-to-use option is the emergency plan game. It is one of the easiest problem-solving activity games to use since its only requirement is space. In this case, the game is more interesting and easier to facilitate and engage in if the room is filled with more objects.

To play this game, gather everyone into a room. Your normal office works just fine if everyone is there. The team must find 10 items they will need to survive being locked in the room for several days. Give the team a set amount of time to discuss it, 30 minutes at the most, then review the team's answers. Everyone on the team must agree to the ten items and rank them in order of importance. This game helps the team improve their communications skills. The team will have to agree on a final answer to win. So, team members will have to communicate their reasoning to the rest of the team in order for the team to win.

The Communication Game

The communication game is another option if you don't want to leave your office building. However, it is best played in an open space with a flat floor. The purpose of the game is to help team members learn to communicate more effectively.

You can play this game with common materials found around the office. It would be advisable to find a set of items that are the size of a fist or a hockey puck, are easy to see at a distance and won't be hard for someone to keep their balance if they step on one. If these items aren't available, you could also play with pieces of colored paper. You will also need enough blindfolds for half of the group.

To play the game, divide the team into groups of two. One person in each group puts on a blindfold. Then, the team leader spreads the set of objects across the floor so no one can walk directly to the other side of the room. Each pair of staff members works together to get the one with the blindfold on across the room without touching the objects. They will have to communicate effectively since the person without the blindfold can't move or touch the other person.

Employers seek people who can handle the minor irritations and the major problems that are a part of every business. What do you do when a customer comes to you with a problem? Can you help when your work team runs into production problems? Could you help save your company from losing its competitive edge? No matter where your career leads you, you'll move faster and higher up the ladder of success if you're perceived as an effective problem solver.

This chapter covers the following valuable problem-solving skills:

- Building a reputation as a problem solver, using skills that you already have, as well as learning to avoid negative problem-solving behaviors
- Using analytical and critical thinking (left brain activities) to analyze and solve problems scientifically
- Solving problems creatively by brainstorming, asking questions, approaching problems from odd angles, note-taking, and visualizing all right brain activities
- Avoiding problem-solving potholes and pitfalls such as logical fallacies, which are errors in rational thought
- Solving problems with the Problem-Solving Process, which involves the following steps:
    o Identifying and defining problems as people, organizational, mechanical, or many-sided in nature
    o Defining goals and objectives
    o Generating solutions by using brainstorming techniques such as word association, clustering, and freewriting
    o Developing a plan of action
    o Following through on a problem-solving plan by planning for contingencies, troubleshooting, learning from mistakes, and maintaining flexibility as you are solving the problem

- Applying problem-solving skills to the decision-making process

Problem-Solving Skills You Already Use

- Identify the problem
- Analyze the problem
- Research
- Brainstorm many options
- Think creatively
- Think logically
- Form a hypothesis
- Select the best option
- Negotiate possible pitfalls
- Troubleshoot

EMPLOYEE APPROACHES TO PROBLEMS

Richmond, a Midwest retailer for 40 years, believes he can tell what kind of career someone will have by the way he or she approaches a problem. Richmond divides would-be problem solvers into five groups:

- **Not my problem.** These employees ignore customers and company problems as if those problems didn't touch them personally. If they do manage to get a job, they probably won't keep it long.

- **Don't ask me**. Some people can't do simple calculations, keep a checkbook or a receipt record, or do basic math. Few employers have the time or means to teach these basic skills.

- **What now?** Some well-meaning employees can't seem to mature into independent problem solvers. They don't trust their own judgment. As a result, they bother somebody every two minutes with a problem too big for them to handle. If these employees don't change their ways and take personal responsibility for decision making, they may annoy themselves out of a job.

- **Straight liner**. Straight liners know how to solve straightforward problems. They can do math and calculations and may be highly skilled professionals. But if the situation requires a new solution or any creativity, they can't handle it. They may keep their job and find a comfortable place in the company. But they shouldn't expect to advance to high levels of management.

- **Creative problem solver**. Businesses will always have spots for people who can use their creativity to solve problems. Creative problem solvers make themselves irreplaceable.

The best tool you have at your disposal for solving problems is your mind. Problem solving begins with clear thinking. And thinking comes in two varieties: scientific and creative.

TIPS FOR TEAM BUILDING WITH PROBLEM-SOLVING ACTIVITIES

Here are some strategies you can use to ensure productive team building sessions:

- **Be realistic about participant abilities:** When developing your own problem-solving activities for team building, be realistic about participant abilities. Everyone brings a specific set of skills to the group, so utilizing everyone's unique traits can ensure the most effective team-building sessions. For instance, if you have a team member who is stronger at motivating others, assign them to a leadership role in the activity.
- **Evaluate your team-building budget:** If you are planning team-building activities, evaluate your team-building budget. The overall costs of team building depend on the activities. For example, off-site activities cost more. However, these activities do not need to be expensive to be effective. There are many free team-building activities you can try in-house or off-site based on your team's needs and preferences.
- **Keep team-building sessions short:** Try to keep team-building sessions short for several reasons. Primarily, short team-building sessions are less intrusive to the work schedule. A session that is 30 minutes long takes away less time than a longer session and is much easier to schedule. That way, you can incorporate it into your routine.

PROBLEM-SOLVING STEPS

Here are the basic steps involved in problem-solving:

1. Define the problem

The first step is to analyze the situation carefully to learn more about the problem. A single situation may solve multiple problems. Identify each problem and determine its cause. Try to anticipate the behavior and response of those affected by the problem. Then, based upon your preliminary observation, use the following tips to pinpoint the problem more accurately:

- Separate facts from opinions
- Determine the process where the problem exists
- Analyze company policies and procedures
- Discuss with team members involved in order to gather more information
- Define the problem in specific terms
- Gather all the necessary information required to solve the problem

While defining a problem at this stage, make sure you stay focused on the problem rather than trying to define it in terms of a solution. For example, "We need to rewrite the training documents" focuses on the solution rather than the problem. Instead, saying, "Training documents are inconsistent" is a better way to define a problem. Depending upon the complexity of the problem, you may want to use tools, like flowcharts and cause-and-effect diagrams, to help define the problem and its root causes.

2. Identify alternative solutions

Brainstorm all possible ways to solve the existing problem. Invite suggestions from everyone affected by it and consult those who may have more experience with the type of challenge you're experiencing. You can also use surveys and discussion groups to generate ideas. Keep the following points in mind while exploring alternatives:

- Consider every aspect that could slow down the process of solving the existing problem
- Make sure the ideas generated are consistent with relevant goals and objectives
- Check that everyone participates in the process of idea generation

- Distinguish between short- and long-term alternatives
- Write down all the proposed solutions. You should have at least five to eight possible solutions for each problem.

3. Evaluate solutions

Now it's time to evaluate your list of alternatives. Assess the positive and negative consequences of each alternative defined in the previous step. Analyze and compare all the alternatives in terms of the resources required for their implementation, including time, data, personnel and budget.

4. Select a solution

After the evaluation process, select a solution most likely to solve the problem. Consider to what extent a solution meets the following objectives:

- It solves the problem smoothly without creating another problem
- It is acceptable to everyone involved
- It is practical and easy to implement
- It fits within the company's policies and procedures

It is important to consider implementation when choosing a solution. Decide the following:

- The employees responsible for executing the solution
- How the employees will implement the solution
- The amount of time and resources needed

5. Implement the chosen solution

The next step involves implementing the chosen solution, which usually requires you to take the following actions:

- Develop an action plan to implement the chosen solution
- Define objectives and separate them into measurable targets to monitor the implementation
- Define timelines for implementation
- Communicate the plan to everyone involved
- Develop feedback channels to use during the process

6. Monitor progress and make adjustments

Make sure to continuously measure progress to ensure your solution works. Gather data and feedback to determine if the solution meets the needs of all those involved. You may need to make adjustments if anything unexpected arises. If you feel the solution doesn't work as planned, you may need to return to your alternative solutions and implement a new plan.

Chapter 13 : INTERPERSONAL SKILLS

Communication is an important part of most industries, especially those in which you work with a team or members of the public. Known as interpersonal skills, the ability to do so successfully might help you get a job or succeed in the one you have. Developing good interpersonal skills might even help support your career satisfaction. In this article, we explain the importance of interpersonal skills in the workplace and provide steps you can use to hone your own abilities, to help you succeed in your career.

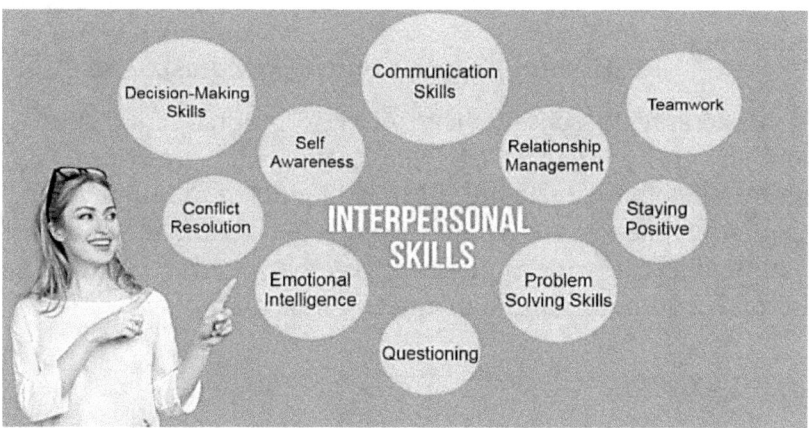

WHAT ARE INTERPERSONAL SKILLS IN THE WORKPLACE?

Interpersonal skills are the abilities you can leverage to interact and communicate with others successfully. In the workplace, this often directly applies to interactions with supervisors, colleagues and members of the public such as customers and clients. People frequently use their interpersonal skills when communicating about their thoughts and ideas for instance, brainstorming a solution to a challenge at work and their feelings and emotions, such as when a team member might praise a colleague or engage in conflict resolution. Many employers value interpersonal skills because they can help teams operate more efficiently and effectively. This, in turn, can have many positive outcomes such as a more enjoyable workplace environment, higher sales and even increased revenues and profits. Strong interpersonal skills may be a part of your personality, and they can also be learned through mindful attention and practice.

What are Interpersonal skills?

Interpersonal skills also known as people skills are the soft skills you use to communicate with and understand others. You use these skills daily when interacting with people face-to-face. Examples of interpersonal skills include:

- Active listening
- Teamwork
- Responsibility
- Dependability
- Leadership
- Motivation
- Flexibility
- Patience
- Empathy
- Conflict resolution
- Negotiation

Many interpersonal skills involve communication. That communication can be verbal such as persuasion or tone of voice or nonverbal such as listening and body language.

INTERPERSONAL SKILLS THAT ARE IMPORTANT AT WORK

While all interpersonal skills can benefit people in the workplace, interpersonal communication is key to working as a team and reaching shared goals. Here are six interpersonal communication skills that are particularly significant at work.

Verbal Communication

Your ability to speak clearly, confidently and appropriately for the situation can help you communicate effectively with others. Choose the correct tone and vocabulary for your audience. For instance, speak formally and professionally during meetings and presentations. Avoid using complex or technical language when trying to explain things or when talking to customers. Ask questions when you need to clarify information.

Active Listening

Active listening is the ability to pay full attention to someone when they speak and to truly understand what they are saying. You are engaged with the speaker and show that by giving verbal and nonverbal responses, including eye contact, nodding and smiling. Active listening also involves paying attention not just to what someone is saying but also to their body language and visual cues. Ask and answer questions to show that you are listening and interested. Active listening is important for communicating effectively and preventing misunderstandings at work. It allows you to understand the information or instructions your coworkers or manager give you. It can also encourage colleagues to share their ideas and collaborate.

Body Language

Your posture, expression and gestures can say just as much as your words. When communicating with coworkers and managers, practice open body language to encourage trust and positivity.

Open body language includes nodding, maintaining eye contact, smiling and being relaxed. Avoid closed body language such as crossed arms, restless behavior and shifting your eyes.

Empathy

Empathy, also known as emotional intelligence, is the ability to understand others' emotions, needs and ideas from their point of view. People who are empathetic have awareness and compassion when communicating. Empathy in the workplace can be good for morale and productivity and can help prevent misunderstandings between employees. By showing empathy, you are more likely to gain your colleagues' trust and respect.

Conflict Resolution

You can use your interpersonal communication skills to help resolve issues and disagreements in the workplace, whether they involve you and a colleague or other parties. This might involve skills such as negotiation, persuasion and understanding both sides of the argument. Listen closely to everyone involved and try to find a solution that benefits all of you. Good conflict resolution skills can lead to a more positive and collaborative work environment. They can also earn you respect and trust from your colleagues.

Teamwork

Groups of employees who can communicate and work well together have a better chance of success and achieving common goals. Being a team player can help you avoid conflict and improve productivity. Do so by offering to help your coworkers when needed and asking them for their feedback and ideas. When team members do give their opinions or advice, listen and react positively. Be encouraging and optimistic when working on projects or in meetings.

HOW TO IMPROVE YOUR INTERPERSONAL SKILLS

If you want to improve your own interpersonal skills, here are some steps you can use:

Establish Your Goals

Setting meaningful goals is an important first step for improving your interpersonal skills. Consider your strengths and specifically what elements of your interactions you'd like to develop. For instance, you might notice that you are adept at initiating conversations with new people but that you find following up to be challenging. Try using the SMART goal framework, meaning you develop goals that are specific, measurable, attainable, relevant and time-based.

SMART is an acronym that stands for specific, measurable, achievable, relevant and time-based. Each element of the SMART framework works together to create a goal that is carefully planned, clear and trackable.

You may have set goals in the past that were difficult to achieve because they were too vague, aggressive or poorly framed. Working toward a poorly crafted goal can feel daunting and unachievable. Creating SMART goals can help solve these problems. Whether you're setting personal or professional goals, using the SMART goal framework can establish a strong foundation for achieving success.

Below, we'll demonstrate how to turn a goal like "I want to be in leadership" into a SMART goal. The words in bold describe your goals.

S = Specific

Be as clear and specific as possible with what you want to achieve. The narrower your goal, the more you'll understand the steps necessary to achieve it.

Example: *"I want to earn a position managing a development team for a startup tech company."*

M = Measurable

What evidence will prove you're making progress toward your goal? For example, if your goal is to earn a position managing a development team for a startup tech company, you might measure progress by the number of management positions you've applied for or interviews you've completed. Setting milestones along the way will give you an opportunity to re-evaluate and course-correct as needed. When you achieve your milestones, remember to reward yourself in small but meaningful ways.

Example: *"I will apply to three open positions for the manager of a development team at a tech startup."*

A = Achievable

Have you set an achievable goal? Setting goals, you can reasonably accomplish within a certain timeframe will help keep you motivated and focused. Using the above example of earning a job managing a development team, you should know the credentials, experience and skills necessary to earn that position. Before you begin working toward a goal, decide whether it's something you can achieve now or whether there are additional preliminary steps you should take to become better prepared.

Example: *"I will update my resume with relevant qualifications, so I can apply to three open positions for the manager of a development team at a tech startup."*

R = Relevant

When setting goals for yourself, consider whether they are relevant. Each of your goals should align with your values and larger, long-term goals. If a goal doesn't contribute toward your broader objectives, you might rethink it. Ask yourself why the goal is important to you, how achieving it will help you and how it will contribute toward your long-term goals.

Example: *"To achieve my goal of being in leadership, I will update my resume with relevant qualifications so I can apply to three open positions for the manager of a development team at a tech startup."*

T = Time-based

What is your goal time frame? An end-date can help provide motivation and help you prioritize. For example, if your goal is to earn a promotion to a more senior position, you might give yourself six months. If you haven't achieved your goal by then, take time to consider why. Your timeframe might have been unrealistic, you might have run into unexpected roadblocks or your goal might have been unachievable.

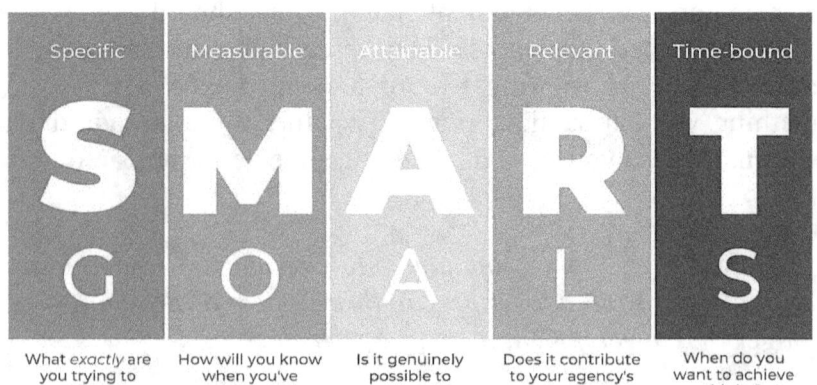

Example: *"To achieve my goal of being in leadership, I will update my resume with relevant qualifications so I can apply to three open positions for the manager of a development team at a tech startup this week."*

Example of SMART Goals

I will obtain a job as a high school math teacher within three months after graduating with my Bachelor of Science in Education degree.

Specific: The goal of becoming a high school math teacher is well-defined.

Measurable: Success can be measured by the number of applications, interviews and job offers.

Achievable: The goal-setter will have the appropriate degree for the job.

Relevant: The goal-setter is planning to get a job in the education industry after getting an education degree.

Time-based: The goal-setter has set a deadline to achieve their objective within the three months following graduation.

Observe Successful Interactions

Try to observe other people successfully interacting with team members, supervisors and customers or clients. Notice specifically what makes those interactions so successful. For instance, you might notice their tone, body language or word choice in a particular situation. Consider sharing your goals with a team member and asking questions to clarify their choices in the interactions you've observed.

Identify ways to practice

Next, brainstorm ways to practice your own skills and abilities. You might seek out a mentor for developing your interpersonal skills, for example, and ask that person to engage in exercises such as role-play scenarios. If you find a mentor, you might also ask them to provide feedback on your interpersonal skills. You might also consider attending formal training sessions focused on interpersonal skills. Consider asking your employer if they provide opportunities for this kind of development, or use your professional network or relevant organizations to independently find the courses you're looking for.

Solicit feedback

Whether you are working with a mentor or in a group training environment, try asking for feedback on your interpersonal skills if it makes sense to do so. Try asking specific questions about scenarios and interactions to help you progress as effectively as possible.

Reflect and Modify

Periodically pause to reflect on the growth and development of your interpersonal skills. Consider setting a reminder or adding a note on your calendar to intentionally perform a self-evaluation or assessment, perhaps. Be sure to think about what skills have improved as well as things that you may continue working on. Modify your strategies if it will support your progress. You might even consider adjusting your goals as your abilities progress.

INTERPERSONAL COMMUNICATION

Interpersonal communication is the process of sharing ideas and emotions verbally and nonverbally with another person. It allows us to interact with and understand others in our personal and professional lives. In the workplace, hiring managers often look for employees with strong interpersonal skills who will collaborate and communicate well with their colleagues. In this article, we will describe the importance of interpersonal skills in your career.

INTERPERSONAL CONFLICT

Interpersonal conflict in the workplace is a natural part of colleague interaction. Conflict can occur between colleagues, within a team or between team members and leaders. If you're experiencing workplace conflict, learning how to resolve it can help you improve your communication skills and become more productive.

TYPES OF INTERPERSONAL CONFLICT

Interpersonal conflict is any type of conflict that involves two or more people. Workplace conflicts arise whenever two or more people express different points of view. This can happen between co-workers, managers or clients and customers. To understand interpersonal conflicts and how best to approach a resolution, it's important to consider every type. Here are the four types of interpersonal conflicts:

Pseudo-conflicts

Pseudo-conflicts arise when two parties want different things and can't come to an agreement. If two team leaders are working on a project but one wants everyone to take notes on a computer and the other wants everyone to use pen and paper, this would be a pseudo-conflict. Their desire to approach a project in two different ways and failing to see eye-to-eye is the reason for the conflict.

Policy-related interpersonal conflict

When conflict relates to a decision or situation that involves both parties, it can be a policy-related interpersonal conflict. For example, if a leader assigns a work project to a team, the members of the team may disagree on the best way to complete it. When policy-related interpersonal conflicts arise in the workplace, it's best to resolve them through compromise.

Value-related interpersonal conflicts

Sometimes conflicts occur between two people when they have different underlying value systems. This kind of conflict can be hard to identify when it first occurs because the people who are in the conflict often think the other party is being stubborn or disagreeable, wherein they just have different underlying values. One colleague may put such a high value on their time outside of the office that they refuse to check e-mails or be reachable during non-office hours.

Ego-related interpersonal conflicts

In ego conflicts, losing the argument has the potential to damage a person's pride. Sometimes ego conflicts arise when many small conflicts are unresolved. One example of ego-related interpersonal conflict results is if one co-worker is already sensitive about a manager favoring another employee. If the manager then asks both parties for their opinion, the co-worker who is already sensitive about the manager favoring the other employee might say or represent his or her bigger feelings about the manager's favoring. This would escalate the conflict further than the situation might warrant.

POTENTIAL RESOLUTION METHODS

The first step to addressing interpersonal conflict is choosing a resolution method. The method you choose can vary depending on the specific conflict and those involved. These are some resolution strategies you can choose from:

Withdrawal

Withdrawal avoids conflict, and this method may be helpful for intense conflicts or minor disagreements that may not warrant thorough discussions. For example, it may not be productive to argue with a co-worker about whether hot or iced coffee is better.

Accommodation

Accommodation is a conflict resolution method in which you consider the other person's needs over your own. For example, you may enact accommodation in a conflict over an office re-design by letting a colleague make the color scheme decisions.

Competition

Those who choose the competition resolution strive to convince others to see why their perspective is best. For example, during a road construction project, you may argue for more safety measures and provide safety data to support your claim.

Compromise

When you choose compromise, both parties work to find a solution that satisfies everyone. For example, during the office re-design, your colleague may choose the color scheme while you choose the new furniture.

Collaboration

Though collaboration often takes more time and effort than other resolution methods, it may provide more long-term benefits.

When your team has the time, choosing collaboration can help build relationships and communication skills.

What Is Conflict Resolution?

Conflict resolution is the process of resolving a dispute between two or more people. Conflict can occur between individual coworkers, between managers, between a manager and a member of their team or between a service provider and a customer or client. It can also occur between groups of people, such as between management and their workforce or between entire departments. When a dispute arises, the best course of action is to use negotiation to resolve the problem. Through negotiation, you can resolve the problem quickly, identify a solution all parties agree to and improve the relationship between the groups in conflict.

Why Is Conflict Resolution Important?

Conflict resolution is essential to maintaining a productive workforce and high workplace morale. Through conflict resolution, you can:

- Understand more about the ideas, backgrounds and beliefs of another person and gain a new perspective that may even change your own.

- Better ensure that relationships continue and grow in the future.

- Find peaceful solutions to everyday challenges and put valuable resources like time, energy, reputation and motivation to better use in the workplace.

HOW татЕ RESOLVE CONFLICT IN THE WORKPLACE

Here are some steps you can use to resolve conflict in your own workplace:

Understand the conflict

Before you begin communicating with the other party, fully understand your position in the conflict and the position of the other party. It's also important to clarify your own interests and those of the other person. Think about what it is that you really care about in the conflict, what your concerns are and what you would like to see happen. Go through the same exercise, thinking about the conflict from the other party's perspective. Think through what agreements you might be able to reach.

Explore alternatives

In some cases, the parties are not able to reach an agreeable solution in a conflict. You need to take this into consideration before you sit down with the other party to resolve the issue. Think about at what point you will walk away from the conflict and what you will do if you can't reach an agreement. Then when you're brainstorming possible resolutions to the conflict, you can compare each of those solutions to the best alternative that you have already decided upon and rapidly determine if the new solution is better.

Find a private, neutral place

It's important to find a quiet and neutral location where you can discuss the conflict in private. Because the goal, ultimately, is to eliminate tension, a private location is essential. A manager's office or even in a conference room may work well if you can close the doors and speak privately without being interrupted.

Communicate both sides

Once you have thought through your interests and those of the other party and have located a private, neutral place in which you can speak, it's time to communicate with one another directly. Here are some tips you can use to make the most of that time together:

- Be an active listener. Listen actively, rephrasing the statement in your own words to ensure you fully understand what the other party is saying. For example, you could start with, "So you're saying that... Did I understand you correctly?"

- Let everyone participate. If there are multiple parties involved in the conversation, allow everyone who wants to contribute to the conversation to do so. People who participate will have a say in how the conflict is resolved and will be helpful in identifying a solution.

- Avoid forming assumptions. Keep an open mind, asking questions and gathering information so that you fully understand each position.

- Remain calm. Remain calm, even if the other party becomes emotional. You may even want to apologize if it's warranted, as it can help diffuse the situation.

Be aware of body language

Be mindful of your body language, as you're conveying information to the other party without even having to speak. You want to project calmness and open-mindedness. Some ways to do this are to:

- Maintaining eye contact
- Being conscious of your expression
- Relaxing your neck and shoulders
- Using a neutral tone with a moderate speed and volume
- Avoiding the use of words that imply an absolute such as "always" or "never"

Identify a common goal

In this step, both parties agree on the desired outcome for the conflict. Once everyone has moved past the root cause of the problem, they often discover that they are working towards the same goal, they just have different opinions on how to reach that goal. Discuss what you would like to see happen and what your interests are. Invite the other party to do the same. Once you've identified the common goal, you can start working towards a resolution.

Use a third-party mediator

In some cases, it may be useful to use a neutral third party whom everyone trusts to be fair. This can help ensure both parties understand one another fully and, if necessary, continually remind everyone of the ultimate goal so that the conversation and brainstorming session remains productive. Some possible jobs for the mediator are:

- Listening to both sides and explaining their positions to each other

- Finding common interests
- Keeping both parties focused, respectful and reasonable
- Looking for solutions that would be considered a win-win for both parties

Brainstorm solutions

Now that you fully understand the conflict, the interests of each party and the common goal for all parties, you can start thinking about possible solutions. Try to come up with as many ideas as possible. Look for win-win solutions or compromises that all parties can agree upon.

Discuss each idea. Consider what's involved and whether the idea involves other people who should be consulted. If an idea cannot be used, discuss why it won't work. If the conflict is between you and someone who works under you, use their ideas first to increase the personal commitment on their part and make them feel heard.

Agree on a plan of action

Identify different solutions that both you and the other party can accept and see where there is common ground. Ideally, you would identify a solution that's a win-win for everyone involved. However, if this isn't possible, look for an idea that everyone can agree with and commit to.

Chapter 14 : COMMUNICATION SKILLS

Communication Skills is the most important skills across any profession

ELECTRONIC COMMUNICATION

There are many forms of electronic communication today, you can communicate via X (formerly known as Twitter), WhatsApp, e-mail, Skype, short messaging service, Telegram, and many other chat applications.

Electronic communication places new demands on language that leads to interesting variations in written language use. Hailed as a powerful educational resource, the electronic communication medium has not only revolutionized the composing process but has also been found to encourage participation in writing activity.

One reason for this is that e-mail and online chats provide a non-threatening atmosphere in which writers feel less inhibited about expressing themselves, encouraging even timid students who usually refuse to speak in face-to-face discussions to actively participate in online chats. Another reason is that the Web provides an arena for writers to present their work to a real and larger audience that extends beyond classroom and school boundaries. When students realize that they are going to put their work on the Web for readers in the real world, they are motivated to write. The electronic communication medium has been found to increase collaborative writing activities. There are mixed views on whether it has a similar effect on the quantity and quality of writing done by individual students.

Because the electronic communication medium reduces the intimidation factor and offers attractive features, it improves students' attitudes towards writing and practicing the target language and encourages students to produce more text. The quality of all relationships is formed and maintained much more through non-verbal communication than through words, which play a relatively minor part. Becoming skilled in reading and interpreting non-verbal behavior is essential to enhancing effectiveness in all relationships and in helping patients. Learning about our own non-verbal behavior, and using that knowledge to influence how we relate to others will help us to see below the surface and to be more useful and successful in everything we do. Physical, and non-verbal elements of the environment also contribute significantly to the messages that patients receive and to their reactions to healthcare. Blindness to non-verbal behavior is almost complete blindness to the meaning and complexity of all communication, of who other people really are and what they are communicating or trying to conceal.

Communication skills are abilities you use when giving and receiving different kinds of information. While these skills may be a regular part of your day-to-day work life, communicating in a clear, effective and efficient way is an extremely special and useful skill. Learning from great communicators around you and actively practicing ways to improve your communications over time will certainly support your efforts to achieve various personal and professional goals. Communication skills involve listening, speaking, observing and empathizing. It is also helpful to understand the differences in how to communicate through face-to-face interactions, phone conversations and digital communications, like email and social media.

There are four main types of communication you might use on a daily basis, including:

- Verbal: Communicating by way of a spoken language.
- Nonverbal: Communicating by way of body language, facial expressions and vocalics.
- Written: Communicating by way of written language, symbols and numbers.

- Visual: Communication by way of photography, art, drawings, sketches, charts and graphs.

E-MAIL COMMUNICATION

Electronic Mail or e-mail is a system of electronic correspondence by which users send and receive messages over a network of computer and telecommunication links. The message may consist of short notes and greetings, or extensive text files plus graphics and photographic images, video clips or sound. Thus, e-mail is an 'electronic past office'. It lets people communicate even in the absence of the receiver at the other end. It means that you can send e-mail message at any time or whenever you want. The person, to whom you have sent the message, can read the same whenever he wants. Thus, the sender and the receiver don't have to connect themselves at the same time to communicate that particular message.

ADVANTAGES OF E-MAIL

- It permits sending to and receiving messages from others having e-mail address.
- It transmits the message almost immediately. Thus, its speed is very fast.
- It does not require the presence of the receiver of the message at the other end. The message is delivered into his mailbox and it can be checked by the receiver by opening his mailbox at any time.
- It directly reaches the concerned individual's electronic mailbox.
- It ensures a higher degree of secrecy of the message.

- It is a very cheap medium of communication. Hard copy letters and memorandums can often be replaced by electronic mail.
- Message can be sent at any time, day or night, eliminating problems brought about by differences in time zone.
- Identical messages can be sent to many people simultaneously.

E-Mail Etiquettes

- Respond to an e-mail within 24 hours.
- For convenience of receiver, provide clearly worded subject lines for all messages.
- Use short paragraph for gaining reader's attention.
- Be complete and concise.
- Use upper and lower-case letters for clarity purposes.
- Inappropriate and unpleasant words must be avoided.
- Avoid adding many attachments to your message.
- Always apply personal name if your mail system allows it.
- Re-read and proof read the message before sending.
- Use grammar checker before sending.

If you have access to your boss's e-mail account, I would suggest you regularly read the e-mails, even if they deal with them themselves. It is always useful to be well informed and to have a broad picture of what they are doing.

Remember to put a heading in the subject in your e-mail. Everyone gets so much e-mail and may scan their in-box for ones they feel they need to read urgently, so make the heading something that will entice them to open it and read it. They may use also the subject heading to file their e-mails by. It is important to remember that if you pick up an e-mail to reply to it, you need to change the subject heading if you are emailing about a different subject. E-mails are easy to send but so difficult to retrieve (if at all), and when writing them you should carefully consider the tone and message conveyed. They must be professional, with correct grammar and spelling. You must also make sure they are sent to the correct recipients, with everyone copied in who should be. It is important not to type in capital letters as this is considered to be shouting on e-mail. Also, the human eye finds it easier to read small letters than capitals. If you want to do headings you can make them bold.

Be careful when sending group e-mails that you do not give away people's e-mail addresses against their wishes. You should use blind copy (bcc) to keep the e-mail addresses of each recipient private. Be careful of how you word e-mails and how they read think about how it will come across to the recipient. If you are angry about something don't send off an e-mail in haste: think about it, draft it and go back to it later when you have calmed down; change it or delete it if necessary, and remember it is sometimes better to pick up a phone or meet face to face.

E-mails that are quite curt, short and to the point are sometimes perceived as coming from someone who is abrupt or arrogant. They can irritate some people even though you may be doing it this way because of lack of time. You should write an e-mail, then read it from the reader's point of view imagining how the wording could be interpreted. Messages should always have a greeting at the beginning and be signed off at the end. It is a good idea to use 'signatures', which may include a farewell greeting such as 'kind regards and your full contact details to help the recipients should they want to call you. Similarly, people do not want to receive long e-mails that ramble on but rather ones that are to the point. If it is necessary to give lots of information, this should be attached as a word document rather than in the e-mail itself. Be very careful with sending confidential information in emails as they can be forwarded on and can be read by the company if the authorities so wish. Consider whether it would be better to post or deliver highly confidential material by hand.

Also be aware of your company's e-mail etiquette. Use your personal e-mail address for personal e-mails rather than clogging up the company's inbox with your personal correspondence. Be careful not to use work time for your personal concerns.

COMMUNICATING EFFECTIVELY IN THE WORKPLACE

While there are several communication skills you will use in different scenarios, there are a few ways you can be an effective communicator at work.

Clear and Concise

Making your message as easy to consume as possible reduces the chance of misunderstandings, speeds up projects and helps others quickly understand your goals. Instead of speaking in long, detailed sentences, practice reducing your message down to its core meaning. While providing context is helpful, it is best to give the most necessary information when trying to communicate your idea, instruction or message.

Empathy

Understanding your colleague's feelings, ideas and goals can help you when communicating with them. For example, you might need help from other departments to get a project started. If they are not willing to help or have concerns, practicing empathy can help you position your message in a way that addresses their apprehension.

Assertive

At times, it is necessary to be assertive to reach your goals whether you are asking for a raise, seeking project opportunities or resisting an idea you don't think will be beneficial. While presenting with confidence is an important part of the workplace, you should always be respectful in conversation. Keeping an even tone and providing sound reasons for your assertions will help others be receptive to your thoughts.

Calm and Consistent

When there is a disagreement or conflict, it can be easy to bring emotion into your communications. It is important to remain calm when communicating with others in the workplace. Be aware of your body language by not crossing your arms or rolling your eyes. Maintaining consistent body language and keeping an even tone of voice can help you reach a conclusion peacefully and productively.

ANSWERING THE PHONE

Answer the phone with a smile on your face. The smile can be 'heard' and you will sound happy and pleasant. If you are extremely busy and getting stressed with your work, take a deep breath before you answer the phone to calm you down and make you sound normal and not anxious. Answer the phone promptly don't let it ring more than three times before you answer it. Set yourself a daily challenge to attempt to answer the phone on the first ring so that callers are not kept holding on the line for longer than is necessary, they will appreciate not having their time wasted. This helps exceed expectations when you are consistent. Always be polite, helpful and proactive when dealing with phone calls. Whenever you can, go that extra mile to help the caller or client it always pays off and sometimes it gets back to your boss how helpful you have been. It improves the perception of the company and client relationships as well as your own reputation and relationships.

Always try to help the callers when they ask for your boss. You will often be quite capable of dealing with the call yourself and it is amazing how many times all the caller wants is some information that you can provide. Find out as much information as possible and if appropriate make notes of the call, then inform your boss as soon as possible and get back to the caller. Callers do not always realize that you can do a lot more than just an answering machine so you have to ask probing questions.

COMMUNICATING WITH DIFFERENT CULTURES

Often, we can see the reason behind our own cultural ways and habits, but others may not see them in the same way. The habits, words and gestures of people from different cultures may seem odd and confusing to us. We are increasingly working across cultures and we should be aware and respectful of each other's norms and differing etiquette. If your boss visits another country, research any cultural differences for that country to make sure the boss does not offend anyone. The ritual of shaking hands is especially important and, particularly for women, the dress code. It is a good idea to provide translations of some basic greeting words 'hello, how are you', 'thank you', 'goodbye' and so on. If possible, when planning to do business in other countries it is advisable to try to spend a day or two there beforehand to do some 'on the ground' research. If time affords then suggest this to your boss and schedule it in the diary. Some countries take a much more direct and focused approach than others, while some will require 'small talk' and relationship building before doing business.

Working with different cultures means that there will be a need for clarity in the communications we make and we should watch and listen and learn from others. However, it is worth remembering that respect, openness and courtesy are common to all cultures. Never assume that others think the same. Even people in the same culture may be brought up in a different environment, which makes them differ from each other. Observe people before you do or say anything that may cause misunderstanding or offend another person. Be careful with the English language as it can cause confusion. The meanings of words and phrases may vary in different English-speaking countries such as the UK, Australia, South Africa and the United States.

Body language also means different things in different countries. The common English and American 'thumbs up' (well done) gesture, for example, would be offensive in some countries. Making eye contact, showing the sole of your foot, personal space, sitting down before the other person, reading a business card, and presenting an object with your left hand all these gestures and behaviors can convey very different impressions. Be warned and watch and listen and learn.

WRITTEN COMMUNICATION

Written communication is best suited when the communicator and the receiver are beyond the oral communication medium. The executives in all organizations can maintain effective inter-departmental and intra-departmental connections through messages in written words. The process of communication involves sending a message in written words. Written communication covers all kinds of subject matter like notices, memorandums, reports, financial statements, business letters, etc. This type of communication simply means a process of reducing messages into writing which is extensively used in organizations. Formal communication must always be in writing such as rules, orders, manuals, policy matters etc.

The systematic filing of written communication is one of the important aspects of communication. Filing along with indexing is necessary because of the poor retention power of human beings. The purpose of preserving written messages is to provide necessary information readily and without any delay and when it is needed. However, the following gives the main purpose of writing the messages.

- **Future references:** The limitation of the human mind and poor retention power cannot be overlooked. Written messages can be preserved as records and reference sources. Various media of communication can be filed for future reference. Thus, keeping records is essential for the continuous operation of the business.

- **Avoiding mistakes:** In transmitting messages, earlier records help in reducing mistakes and errors and also prevent the occurrence of fraud.

Legal requirements: Written communication is acceptable as a legal document. That is why some executives think that even if some messages have been transmitted orally, they should later be confirmed in writing.

Wide access: Communication media has become very fast, and written communication enjoys wide access. If the communicator and the receiver are far from each other, written communication sent through post or e-mail is the cheapest and may be the only available means of communication between them.

Effective decision-making: old documents help effective decision-making in a great way. Decision-making process becomes easier if old records are available. Because the messages provide the necessary information for decision-making purpose.

PRESENTATION

Successful presenting consists of three elements:

Content: The presentation should be packed with practical and easy-to-remember information. Inject enthusiasm about the topic into your presentation through your voice and body language. Ask the audience questions so they have to keep awake, think and answer, delegates like to give answers. Also, try to include one or two exercises to get them thinking and joining in. Keep your presentation to the point and practice it to make sure that it lasts the length of time you are allotted to speak, taking into consideration question-and-answer time if appropriate. Always remember that you may miss out on something you intended to say but the audience will never know that you missed it so don't worry about it. Tell short stories to bring your presentation to life (these may be humorous) but be careful about telling jokes as they can seem out of place.

Confidence: Remember that some people get nervous in audiences too. You can put them at their ease by showing with your body language that you are confident of your ability; let them realize they will enjoy the forthcoming presentation. Knowing that you have information to share that is valuable for others also gives you confidence and satisfaction. Confidence will come with practice and with performing and being successful.

Practice: It is extremely important to write your presentation and practice, practice, practice until you can give it with ease. It is a well-known fact that the audience will only remember 7 percent of the words you say; 93 percent of what they will remember is your attitude, tone of voice and your physical presentation skills.

Once you know your presentation thoroughly, you then have to concentrate on how to give it in the most effective and memorable way you can. Make a connection with the audience by eye contact and drawing them into the message you wish to give by making it alive and interesting. Then the audience will be listening to every word and waiting to hear what you have to say next. You can use your experiences and anecdotes to help people remember the points you are making. You can also use a mnemonic to link key messages together.

PRESS CONFERENCE

Press conference is called when an organization has something newsworthy to tell to the media, and when more in-depth approach and discussion is needed then it is possible to provide by sending out a press release. There are two major reasons for holding a news conference. One is so that a newsmaker who gets many questions from reporters can answer them all at once rather than answering dozens of phone calls. Another is so someone can try to attract news coverage for something that was not of interest to journalists before. In a news conference, one or more speakers may make a statement, which may be followed by questions from reporters. Sometimes only questioning occurs, sometimes there is a statement with no questions permitted. Press conference gives reporters a possibility to ask questions, get explanations, quotes, and photo opportunity. While organizing press conference following points should be kept in the mind:

An invitation to the conference should be sent to reporters and desk editors a week ahead of it. Closer to the date a day or two before it a phone call can be made to remind the reporters on the event.

You should organize press conference between 9-11 in morning or 4-7 in evening. Later then or before that is not good - reporters will not have time to file a story for the next day newspaper issue.

Ideally, the conference will have several persons participating: the press officer who knows the reporters will open and facilitate it. One or two prominent persons should be present, who will give a 10-min statement each on the issue (project, release, donation, opening, or similar), after which the facilitator will give floor to the reporters to ask questions. All in all, ideally it should be finished in 45 min. After that individual interviews can be given.

A "press kit" is usually distributed at a conference, containing a press release, background of organizers, report, research results, fact sheets, list of experts, etc. Sometimes even filmed material or photo material is distributed. After the conference you should send the press kit by a messenger to those media outlets that have not sent a representative at the conference.

Reporters like to say that "A press conference should scream for a headline" meaning there should be breaking news released on them. If a conference is called and there is no such news, journalists will not forget it. There is a chance that next time, even if you have breaking news, nobody will show up at the event.

Exactly because of the proliferation of press conferences, media outlets often send beginners to cover them.

If possible, media events should be organized instead of press conference. Yet, if one decides to organize a press conference, there are a number of technical details to be taken care of.

Conference

A conference is closed group discussion. A conference is usually a large gathering of persons who meet to confer on a particular theme or to exchange experience or information. A conference may be held to exchange views on some problem being faced by the organization or some other issue related to it, and it may even suggest a solution, but the suggestions from a conference are not binding. They are more in the nature of recommendations. The participants in the conference have to register for attending the conference.

Within the organization, the sales manager may hold a weekly conference of the salesmen to review sales during the week and to plan the next week's strategy on the basis of the views expressed by them. Conference may sometimes be held to give training to new employees. These employees may be exposed to a conference where necessary information about the organization is imparted to them and through discussion in an informal atmosphere, they are made to learn all about the organization, its objectives, policies, etc. This kind of conference may be described as a conference for training. Occasionally a large industrial concern may take initiative and invite delegates from other similar concerns to a conference to discuss problem of mutual interest. The host organization selects the venue of the conference, makes arrangements for the stay of the delegates, chalks out detailed program, invite eminent people to chair various sessions, selects the speakers, and at the end of the conference sends out reports to leading newspapers highlighting some of the important aspects of the conference.

GLOSSARY

Acceptance testing   Formal testing conducted to determine whether or not a system satisfies its pre-defined acceptance criteria, and to enable the customer to determine whether or not to accept the system.

Accepted   The recorded decision or formal sign-off by the customer that an output or sub-output has satisfied the documented requirements and may be delivered to the customer or used in the next part of the process.

Activity   An element of work performed during the course of a project. (Normally has duration, expected cost, and expected resource requirements.) Also called a work item.

Amount at stake   the extent of adverse consequences which could occur to the project. (Also referred to as risk impact).

Assumption   Assumptions are factors that, for planning purposes, will be considered to be true, real or certain. Assumptions generally involve a degree of risk and also should be reflected in the Risk Management Plan.

Authorized   The recorded decision that a deliverable or output has been cleared for use or action after having satisfied the quality standards for the project.

Baseline Metrics   A set of indicators to set as measures against which to judge and report progress or performance.

Benefits   Refer to *Outcomes*

Business Case   A one-off, start-up document used by corporate management to assess the justification of a proposed project, or to assess the development options for a project that has already received funding. If approved, it confirms corporate management support and/or funding for a recommended course of action.

Business Customer(s)   There may be other Business Units who will utilize the project outputs, but who do not have management responsibility for their ongoing maintenance or for the realization of outcomes/benefits. These are known as the Business Customers. Sometimes the Project Observer or the Project Business Owner(s) represents the interests of the Business Customer(s).

Business Owner(s)   The Business Owner(s) is responsible for managing the project outputs for utilization by the Project Customers. There may be one or more Business Owners, at a number of managerial levels, depending on the size of the project. The Business Owner(s) must be satisfied that the project includes all of the outputs necessary for outcome/benefits realization. Each output must be specified and delivered fit-for-purpose. Usually the Business Owner(s) is accountable to the Project Sponsor or their delegate(s), who may be Senior Management in the Agency, for the realization of project Target Outcomes. One or more Business Owners are usually Steering Committee members. The Business Owner(s) must be identified for all projects, no matter what the size or complexity, even if they are the same entity as the Project Sponsor, or indeed the Project Manager.

Change Control Board   A formally constituted group of stakeholders responsible for approving or rejecting changes to the project baselines.

Constraints   Factors that will limit the project management team's options. For example, a predefined budget, deadlines, technology choices, scope or legislative processes.

Consultant   An organization or individual contracted to provide high-level specialist or professional advice to assist decision-making by management. Consultants will be expected to exercise their own skills and judgment independently.

Contingency Planning   The development of a management plan that identifies alternative strategies to be used if specified risk events occur.

Contingency Reserve The amount of money or time needed above the estimate to reduce the risk of overruns of project objectives to a level acceptable to the organization.

Contract An agreement for provision of goods and/or services, between two or more parties, intended to create a legal obligation between them and to be legally enforceable.

Contractor An organization or individual contracted to provide a specialize service. A contractor will usually work under the supervision of an Agency Manager to provide services that are not readily available.

Corporate Client The high-level champion of the project who has ultimate authority. They promote the benefits of the project to the community.

Corporate Goals The goals or objectives identified by the organization to support the core business of that organization.

Cost of Conformance The cost of conforming to Specifications, Planning, Training, Control, Validation, Test, and Audits.

Cost Benefit Analysis The economic and social justification for a proposed project.

Critical Path The chain of activities that link the start to the finish of the project, and for which any delay will cause the project to be delayed by the same amount of time. The longest time taken to complete a project activity is the critical path.

Customer(s) See *Project Customer(s)*

Decision Tree Analysis A diagram that describes a decision under consideration and the implications of choosing one or another of the available alternatives. It incorporates probabilities or risks and the costs or rewards of each logical path of events and future decisions.

Deliverable A tangible, verifiable work output, such as a Feasibility Study, a detailed design, a working prototype, any report, manual, specification, programming or other output, developed as part of a project. Usually a component of a high-level output descriptor.

Document Control   All documents, whether electronic or hard copy, need to be uniquely identifiable. In most cases, it is also necessary to track the changes that occur to the document and record its distribution throughout the document's development and subsequent revision(s).

Document control includes:

- The use of version numbers on documents (version control)
- Maintaining a history of the development of versions (build status)
- The use of numbered copies of documents (controlled documents)
- Maintaining a list of recipients for distributed copies (distribution list)

Expected Monetary Value   The product of an event's probability of occurrence and the gain or loss that will result.

Expected Monetary Value = Money at Risk x Probability.

For example, if there is a 50% probability it will rain, and rain will result in a $100 loss, the expected monetary value of the rain event is $50 (.5 * $100).

Fast Tracking   Compressing the project schedule by overlapping activities that would normally be done in sequence (such as design and construction).

Feasibility Report   A report that is developed as a result of a Feasibility Study, and is presented to senior management to determine whether a project has sufficient merit to continue into more detailed phases.

Refer to Feasibility Study

Feasibility Study   A study to assess the viability of a potential project. It includes a cost/benefit analysis and results in the development of a Feasibility Report.

Refer to Feasibility Report

Fitness-for-purpose   the features by which the quality of an output is determined. In other words, what criteria will be used to test whether the outputs meet the needs of the project's Business Owner(s) and Customers, and will in turn enable outcomes to be realized

Gantt Chart   Horizontal bar charts that can graphically depict   the time relationship of tasks, activities and resources in a project.

Goals   Refer to Objectives

Governance   The management structure created for the life of a project.

Refer to Governance Model and Governance Structure

Governance Model   A generic model that indicates the people most likely to be incorporated in a project governance structure. It is also an indication of some of the ways in which the people would be most likely to interact.

Implementation Plan   Describes how the outputs will be delivered to the Business Owner(s), including any special requirements such as stage implementation or 'roll out', training and delivery requirements.

ISO Standards   the International Standards Organization (ISO) has developed a set of international standards that can be used in any type of business, and are accepted around the world as proof that a business can provide assured quality.

Issue A   concern raised by any stakeholder that needs to be addressed, either immediately or during the project. As issues are reviewed during the project, they may become a threat to the project and a mitigation strategy prepared. They are usually documented in a Project Issues Register.

IPO Model   Input-Process-Output model. It is an effective model that helps to define the inputs into a particular project management process to produce the actual outputs of that process.

Management Reserve   A separately planned quantity used to allow for future situations which are impossible to predict. Management reserves are intended to reduce the risk of missing cost or schedule objectives. Use of management reserves requires a change to the project's cost baseline. Management reserves are not included in the project's cost and schedule baseline. Also used to manage "unknown unknowns" types of risk.

Milestone A   significant scheduled event that acts as a progress marker in the life of a project. A milestone is either passed or it is not, the achievement or non-achievement of which is monitored and reported.

Mitigation   Taking steps to lessen risk by lowering the probability of a risk event's occurrence or reducing its effect should it occur

Non-Key Stakeholder(s)   Stakeholders who do not need to be recognized in order for the project to be successful, but who will be identified as a result of the process of identifying all stakeholders.

Outcome(s)   The benefits and other long-term changes that are sought from undertaking a project. Project outcomes are achieved from the utilization of the outputs delivered by a project.

Output(s)   The services or products resulted from a Process. It is delivered to the Business Owner(s) by the project.

Performance Measures   Criteria for measuring a project's success, whether the project is under control and the level of adherence to documented plans, methodologies and standards.

Phase A section of work in a project for which there are no measurable outcomes at the end, although some outputs may be produced. Large and/or complex projects often scope the work in phases to enable each phase to be planned in more detail on completion of the previous phase.

Post Implementation Review A review of a completed project. It may be a review of one or more aspects of the project. For example, whether the outcomes (benefits) were realized, the fitness-for-purpose of the outputs produced or the project and quality management processes selected and applied.

Project A group of related projects that are managed in a coordinated fashion to support the organization strategic goals. E.g., a transformation program comprised of several projects that are implemented together to achieve the project objectives.

Project A project brings about change and involves a group of inter-related activities that are planned and then executed in a certain sequence, to create a unique product or service (output) within a specific timeframe so that outcomes are achieved.

Project Issues Register A list of all issues, details of how these issues are being managed and their current status.

Project Risk Management Includes the processes concerned with identifying, analyzing, and responding to project risk.

Project Customer(s) The person or entities that will utilize the project outputs to generate the outcomes. See also Business Owner and Business Customer

Project Charter A formal document issued by senior management which explains the purpose of the project including the business need the project addresses and the resulting product. It provides the project manager with the authority to apply organizational resources to project activities.

Project Brief Project Brief is a specific purpose document outlining what is to occur in the Initiation Phase of a project. A Project Brief is particularly useful where an output, which will result in a decision to proceed or not with the proposed project, is to be delivered from this initial phase. It also may be used instead of a small Project Business Plan for small projects.

Project Business Case   Refer to Business Case

Project Business Plan The high-level management document for the project. It is owned, maintained and utilized by the Steering Committee to ensure the delivery of project outputs and the realization of defined project outcomes.

Project Execution Plan   The 'road map' used by the Project Team to deliver the agreed project outputs. It outlines the responsibilities of the Project Team and stakeholders.

Project Management Quality Review Consultant   This role involves undertaking independent reviews and reporting to the Project Manager and Steering Committee on whether the management processes involved in the project are appropriate and effective.

Project Management   Project Management is a formalized and structured method of managing change in a rigorous manner. It focuses on achieving specifically defined outputs that are to be achieved by a certain time, to a defined quality and with a given level of resources so that planned outcomes are achieved.

Project Management Framework   The formalized structure, processes and tools employed by an organization or enterprise to the management of all projects.

Project Management Methodology   A pre-defined set of tasks that are designed to provide a guide or a checklist for developing and implementing projects.

Project Management Team   The members of the project team who are directly involved in project management activities. On some smaller projects, the project management team may include virtually all of the project team members.

Project Manager the Project Manager is contracted by the Steering Committee to deliver the defined project outputs.

Project Metrics Measures used to indicate progress or achievement of a project.

Project Observer the Project Observer can be present at Steering Committee meetings or Project Team meetings to act as an information channel to the Agency they are representing. They usually have no voting rights.

Project Outcomes Review A review of a project, involving as many project participants as possible, to assess if the desired outcomes/benefits were attained.

Project Output Review A review of a project, involving as many project participants as possible, to evaluate the fitness-for-purpose of the outputs, the amount of deviation that occurred from the original specifications requested by the customer and the final result, and how any changes to these specifications were managed and approved.

Refer to Project Outcomes Review and Post Implementation Review

Project Phase Refer to Phase

Project Plan Refer to Project Schedule

Project Portfolio Management The management of prioritized projects within the organization, Business Unit, Agency or across government. It is a dynamic process requiring re-prioritization, as necessary, to meet changing business requirements or emerging opportunities.

Project Proposal The initial document that converts an idea or policy into the details of a potential project, including the outcomes/benefits, outputs, major risks, costs, stakeholders and an estimate of the resourcing and time required.

Project Schedule A detailed plan of major project phases, milestones, activities, tasks and the resources allocated to each task. The most common representation of the project schedule is the Gantt Chart.

Refer to Gantt Chart

Project Scope The work that must be done in order to deliver a product with the specified features and functions.

Project Sponsor the Project Sponsor has ultimate accountability and responsibility for the project and is a member of the Steering Committee, usually the Chair. The Sponsor oversees the business management and project management issues that arise outside the formal business of the Steering Committee. The Sponsor also lends support by advocacy at a senior level and ensures that the necessary resources (both financial and human) are available to the project. The Corporate Client and Project Sponsor may be the same person for some projects.

Project Stakeholder An individual or group whose interest in the project must be recognized if the project is to be successful. In particular, those who may be positively or negatively affected during the project or on successful completion the project.

Project Status Report A regular report on the status of the project, with regard to project performance, milestones, budget, issues, risks and areas of concern, to the appropriate people.

Project Team the Project Team is led by the Project Manager working for the successful delivery of the project outputs.

Project Plan A formal, approved document used to guide both project execution and project control. The primary uses of the project plan are to document planning assumptions and decisions, to facilitate communication among stakeholders, and to document approved scope, cost, and schedule baselines.

Quality Assurance 1) The process of evaluating overall project performance on a regular basis to provide confidence that the project will satisfy the relevant quality standards. 2) The organizational unit that is assigned responsibility for quality assurance.

Project Quality Management The processes required to ensure that the project will satisfy the needs for which it was undertaken. Modern quality management complements modern project management in that both recognize the importance of customer satisfaction and prevention over inspection.

Purchasing Plan Provides a detailed plan of the process for acquiring the proposed goods and services to support the delivery of the project's outputs.

Residual Risk A risk that remains after risk responses have been implemented.

Quality Assurance The application of planned, systematic activities, within a documented management framework, that provides confidence that the outputs from a process meet the Business Owner's requirements.

Quality Control The process of monitoring the adherence to documented quality assurance procedures.

Quality Management Quality management is the policy and associated procedures, methods and standards required for the control of projects. The purpose of quality management is to increase certainty by reducing the risk of project failure. It also provides the opportunity for continuous improvement.

Quality Management System Defined policies and procedures that provide a formal framework describing the way an organization conducts its core business. The performance of each quality management procedure generates objective evidence by which to measure the performance of the organization and its management.

Quality Plan Also commonly called the Quality Management Plan. It summarizes the quality management approach and how it will support the delivery of the project outputs.

Reference Group A committee that provides forums to achieve consensus among groups of stakeholders. Often provides expert advice on the development of project outputs. There may be more than one Reference Group for large projects.

Resources The people, finances, physical and information resources required to perform the project activities.

Risk Any factor (or threat) that may adversely affect the successful completion of the project. They are usually documented in a Risk Register.

Refer to Risk Register

Risk Assessment Undertaking a process to assess identified threats to the success of the project, which results in working papers of the current assessment for each threat (both likelihood and seriousness), a risk grading and strategies for mitigating the risks. The results of this analysis are usually captured in the Risk Register.

Refer to Risk Register

Risk Management Describes the processes concerned with identifying, analyzing and responding to project risk. It consists of risk identification, risk analysis, risk evaluation and risk treatment. The processes are iterative throughout the life of the project.

Risk Management Plan Summarizes the proposed risk management approach for the project.

Risk Register A document that records the results of a risk analysis process. It includes the identified threats to the success of the project, the current assessment for each threat (both likelihood and seriousness), a risk grading and strategies for mitigating the risks.

Risk Response Plan A document detailing all identified risks, including description, cause, probability of occurrence, impacts on objectives, proposed responses, owners, and current status. Also known as the risk register.

Scope A clear statement of the areas of impact and boundaries of the project. The scope of a project includes the Target

Outcomes, other benefits, customers, outputs, work and resources (both financial and human).

Scope Statement   A documented description of the project as to its output, approach, and content. (What is being produced? How is it being produced? and What is included?)

Scope creep   Any modification to the scope of a project that has not been authorized or approved by the appropriate individual or group.

Refer to Scope

Slippage   The extent to which the project is falling behind time in relation to the Project Development Schedule.

Stage   A major segment of a project for which there are outputs and outcomes at the end.

Stakeholder Management Plan   Identifies and summarizes stakeholder involvement, including identification of stakeholders for related projects.

Stakeholder   A person or organization that has an interest in the project processes, outputs or outcomes.

Steering Committee   A Project Steering Committee is the key body within the governance structure that is responsible for the business issues associated with the project. It is essential to ensuring the delivery of the project outputs and the achievement of project outcomes/benefits. Its responsibilities include approving the budgetary strategy, defining and realizing benefits, monitoring risks, quality and timelines, making policy and resourcing decisions, and assessing requests for changes to the scope of the project.

Steering Committee Charter   A charter developed for use by Steering Committees for Tasmanian Government projects. The Charter describes the basic role and functions of a Steering Committee, both as a collective group and as individual members.

Refer to Steering Committee

Target Outcome(s) The measurable benefits that are sought from undertaking a project. Target Outcomes are achieved from the utilization of the outputs delivered by a project. Stated, identified targets and measures are developed for gauging progress towards their achievement.

Refer to Outcome(s)

Test Plan A detailed plan that addresses all aspects related to the test of an output or sub-output. It should include test scenarios, the test schedule and define any necessary support tools.

Test Specification Describes the test criteria and the methods to be used in a specific test to assure the performance and design specifications have been satisfied. The test specification identifies the capabilities or project functions to be tested and identifies the test environment. It may include test data to support identified test scenarios.

Testing The process of exercising or evaluating an output, such as an IT system or system component, by manual or automated means, to confirm that it satisfies specified requirements or to identify differences between expected and actual results.

Threat Refer to Risk

Version Control A control or identification system for documents, outputs and sub-outputs, enabling stakeholders to identify readily each different release.

Work Breakdown Structure It refers to the breaking down of the work in a project into related tasks, sometimes described as an Activity Decomposition Chart.

AUTHOR BIOGRAPHY

Dr Zulk Shamsuddin, PhD, AMC®, CIPT, MPM®

Accredited Management Consultant®
Chartered International Professional Trainer
Master Project Manager®

     Dr. Zulk is a technology and business consultant with skills and experience in learning and development, project management, design, and delivery of strategic training programs for knowledge, career development and professional skills certifications. A certified trainer and certification counsellor of The American Academy of Project Management ® AAPM and the Global Academy of Finance and Management ® GAFM. Dr. Zulk is a senior member of the global advisory Board and the International Board of Standards.

Join Dr. Zulk international network at PMI Community

https://community.pmi.org/profile/zulkhernain

www.ingramcontent.com/pod-product-compliance
Lightning Source LLC
Chambersburg PA
CBHW071018240526
45469CB00006BD/1976